We Believe:
The Nicene Creed

—————

BIBLE STUDY

Adriel Sanchez *with*

Josh Maloney

c·c

We Believe: The Nicene Creed
Bible Study
by Adriel Sanchez with Josh Maloney

© 2024 Sola Media
13230 Evening Creek Drive
Suite 220–222
San Diego, CA 92128

Design and Creative Direction by Metaleap Creative
Cover Illustration by Peter Voth

Printed in the United States of America

First Printing November 2023

Contents

Why *This* Study?

Introduction

To begin, we would like to thank you—students, congregants, church leaders, elders, pastors, and churches—for supporting and using this Bible study. We hope it enriches your Christian life, challenges your heart, and builds up your faith to the glory of God.

Why Study the Nicene Creed?

What does the word *Christian* mean? Does it always refer to certain beliefs, or can *Christian* mean whatever we want it to mean? If you're not sure about these questions or just want a clear summary of the core of the Christian faith, then the Nicene Creed is for you. This ancient summary of biblical truth has been passed on for centuries, teaching each new generation the essentials of their faith. It teaches the doctrines that every true church of Christ proclaims about the Triune God—Father, Son, and Holy Spirit—who created and then redeemed the world. The Nicene Creed proclaims the biblical beliefs that the modern church must stand on and treasure.

All of our studies are designed with several things in mind:

1. **TO ADVANCE THE GOSPEL**

   The Pew Research Center reports a rapidly changing religious landscape in the U.S., with the percentage of those identifying as atheist, agnostic, or "nothing in particular" up nine percent in just the last 10 years.[1] Almost 60 percent of our youth leave their churches as young adults, and this number is growing.

   Despite this unsettling news, the core message of Christianity—the gospel—is still capable of renewing our lives and the church.

   Rather than worrying or acting out of fear and self-preservation, the best hope for Christians, the church, and people who feel pressure to abandon their faith is the historic Christian faith, the gospel announcement of what God has done through Jesus Christ for the world.

2. **TO SPEAK TO HONEST QUESTIONS**

   Many in our evangelical, Baptist, Reformed, Lutheran, and Anglican churches have honest questions about faith and life that they may be afraid to ask. We shaped this study to address the concerns of long-time Christians, new Christians, Christians with wavering faith, and skeptics alike.

3. **TO ENGAGE THE DRAMA OF SCRIPTURE, TEACH THE DOCTRINE OF HISTORIC CHRISTIANITY, MOVE US TO DOXOLOGY (WORSHIP), AND ENABLE HEALTHY DISCIPLESHIP**

   Our studies are written to show how doctrine naturally arises out of the Bible's narrative of Jesus Christ and his saving work. We designed the reflection and discussion questions with a practical emphasis to help you engage the material in a prayerful way that should inspire worship and lead to a fuller understanding of how to live as a disciple of Christ.

---

1 Pew Research Center, "In U.S., Decline of Christianity Continues at Rapid Pace: An update on America's changing religious landscape," October 17, 2019, https://www.pewforum.org/2019/10/17/in-u-s-decline-of-christianity-continues-at-rapid-pace/.

4. TO BE USEFUL IN A VARIETY OF SETTINGS

We wrote this study thinking of Sunday school classes, Bible study groups, informal gatherings among friends, and individuals who want to learn more about the Christian faith. Each lesson includes a series of short sections containing a reading and a set of reflection questions. The leader's edition of this study has group discussion questions so that Christians can come together to share insights, ask questions, pray together, and be equipped to share what they're learning with friends and family.

We recommend you work through one lesson per week. If meeting with a group, we suggest reading the lesson and answering the questions on your own first.

"BELOVED, ALTHOUGH I WAS VERY EAGER

TO WRITE TO YOU ABOUT OUR COMMON

SALVATION, I FOUND IT NECESSARY TO

WRITE APPEALING TO YOU TO CONTEND

FOR THE FAITH THAT WAS ONCE FOR ALL

DELIVERED TO THE SAINTS."

Jude 3

What's *the* Rule *of* Faith?

Read 1 John 4:1–3; Galatians 1:6–9

What's a Christian?

Many people around the world call themselves Christians. But is *Christian* just a label? Do we need to believe certain things to truly be a Christian?

Maybe you have convictions about what every Christian must believe. Or maybe you think it's intolerant to say that all Christians need to believe certain things. That's a common attitude in the modern world. Are any of us in the position to say that certain beliefs are truly Christian and that others aren't?

The Heartbeat of the Christian Faith

From its beginning, Christ's church has faced questions about what it really means to be a Christian. In the Bible, we have a record of the first churches and their struggle against people who taught false things about Jesus. These teachers said they believed in Jesus, but what they said about him was wrong.

The apostles—the men Jesus called to the task of establishing his church—had to fight these false teachers (1 John 4:1–3; Col. 2:8–10). The apostles took this responsibility seriously because the stakes were eternal. The apostle Paul told the Galatians, a church that was being led astray, "If we or an angel from heaven should preach to you a gospel contrary to the one we preached to you, let him be accursed" (Gal. 1:8). The apostles knew that sinners could find salvation in Jesus alone. For that reason, the truth about Jesus needed to be taught and protected.

The word *Christian*, then, has always been more than a label. It refers to people who share a set of core beliefs. But what are these beliefs? What must someone believe in order to be a Christian?

In the early church, defenders of biblical Christianity called these core beliefs "the rule of faith." The "rule of faith" referred to the heartbeat of Christianity. It referred to the doctrines, or teachings, that the apostles handed down to the church.

The rule of faith is what we find in the Nicene Creed. This ancient creed is a summary of the core Christian doctrines. They're the essential teachings of the Christian faith. If we don't embrace these truths, we're not within the bounds of historic, orthodox Christianity. We're not within the bounds of biblical faith. We've departed from what the apostles gave to the church.

That's why it's so important for us to study the Nicene Creed. Through this ancient creed, we can understand and embrace the foundations of our faith. By studying this short document that some of our earliest fathers in the faith struggled to create—against great opposition—we can also come to *love* the beliefs we confess.

How Should We Study God?

As we begin this study, our attitude matters. Learning about God isn't like studying an amoeba under a microscope. He's not a *thing* we can observe in a detached way. He's the holy, almighty, and eternal God. He's incomprehensible. That means we can't understand him with our finite minds except in the ways he makes himself known to us. And he's the living God. He created us and gives us every breath we take.

The Bible says, "Let us offer to God acceptable worship, with reverence and awe, for our God is a consuming fire" (Heb. 12:28–29). When we learn theology, the knowledge of God, we come to know of our majestic, sovereign Creator. For that reason, we should approach the topics in this study with "reverence and awe."

Years ago, when I had just started seminary, I took a class called the Doctrine of God. I walked into that class as a young guy training for the ministry and felt excited about what I would learn. The professor had written a lot of books on the doctrine of God. These books focused especially on the doctrines of the Trinity and the Incarnation. I looked up to him. I remember thinking, "Wow, this is going to be awesome. We're going to learn all of these wonderful things straight from this professor."

But as my professor began the class, he said something I'll never forget. He said, "Hey, you guys are here for the doctrine of God. In this class, we're going to talk about things that are majestic, things that are bigger than me. So would you pray for me? Pray that God would give me the strength to be able to talk about these teachings with you."

Those comments really struck me. Here was this guy I looked up to saying, "When we talk about the doctrine of God, it requires a lot of prayer. It requires humility."

So as you begin this study on the Nicene Creed, the rule of faith, pray that God will bring you into a deeper understanding of who he is and what he has done. Pray that God will bless your desire and efforts to know him as you study the great historic truths of the Christian faith.

Questions for Reflection

1. Do you believe it's intolerant to say people are only true Christians if they believe certain doctrines? Why or why not?

2. How do you think we should approach theology, the study of God? How do you think it's similar to and different from learning about other things?

Read Acts 15:1–19; Mark 1:21–25

What Do You Believe?

Every Sunday, before the Lord's Supper, I ask my congregation, "Church, what do you believe?" The church responds by confessing the words of the Nicene Creed:

> I believe in one God, the Father Almighty,
> Maker of heaven and earth, and of all things visible and invisible.
> And in one Lord Jesus Christ, the only begotten Son of God,
> begotten of the Father before all worlds;
> God of God, Light of Light, very God of very God;
> begotten, not made, being of one substance with the Father,
> by whom all things were made.
> Who, for us men and for our salvation,
> came down from heaven
> and was incarnate by the Holy Spirit of the virgin Mary,
> and was made man;
> and was crucified also for us under Pontius Pilate;
> he suffered and was buried;
> and the third day he rose again, according to the Scriptures;
> and ascended into heaven, and sits on the right hand of the Father;
> and he shall come again, with glory, to judge the living and the dead;
> whose kingdom shall have no end.
> And I believe in the Holy Spirit, the Lord and Giver of Life;
> who proceeds from the Father and the Son;
> who with the Father and the Son together is worshipped and glorified;
> who spoke by the prophets.
> And I believe in one holy catholic and apostolic church.
> I acknowledge one baptism for the remission of sins;
> and I look for the resurrection of the dead,
> and the life of the world to come. Amen.

This statement, the Nicene Creed, summarizes "the faith that was once for all delivered to the saints" (Jude 3).

The "saints" aren't special, holy people. Every sinner who has put his or her faith in Christ is a saint. The Nicene Creed summarizes the biblical teaching that Christians are called to embrace with their whole hearts.

That's why the church I serve recites the Nicene Creed every week.

But who created this creed, and why did they write it?

Who Wrote the Nicene Creed?

The Nicene Creed is often called the first ecumenical creed. The word *ecumenical* refers to the whole church gathering together. The Nicene Creed wasn't written by an individual Christian. It also wasn't written by one small group of Christians who wanted to announce their new ideas. Instead, the Nicene Creed was written on behalf of the whole church. Its authors intended to write something that would represent the voice of all God's people. It would be the church's confession of faith—the true faith that Christ entrusted to the apostles.

The Bible shows a model of this kind of church gathering. Acts 15 describes an ecumenical meeting that's often called the Jerusalem Council. At the meeting, the church's leaders met in Jerusalem to address a conflict in the church. They needed to come together to resolve this conflict in a faithful way.

The controversy was about how gentile believers could become part of the church. Most of the first Christians were Jewish, and some of these Jewish Christians said that gentiles who became Christians needed to be circumcised and keep the Old Testament law of Moses. Was that belief true? That's the question the apostles faced when they assembled. Reasoning together under the guidance of the Holy Spirit, they came to a decision: gentiles weren't bound to keep the law of Moses or be circumcised.

The Nicene Creed was written almost 300 years after the Jerusalem Council, in AD 325. The Council of Nicaea, which created the first version of the Nicene Creed, brought together church leaders from all over the Roman Empire. The church faced another major controversy, so the leaders of the church said, "Hey, we need to come together and talk about what's going on. The church is deeply divided over issues that are at the heart of our faith." The apostles were long gone, but the apostolic teaching continued to be threatened.

What, in particular, was the controversy that led to the Nicene Creed?

As we'll see, the Nicene Creed summarizes the core Christian doctrines, but one main question led to the Council of Nicaea. That question was, "Is Jesus really God?"

"Who Do You Say I Am?"

These questions about Jesus aren't old news. By the time the Nicene Creed was written, many people in the Roman Empire claimed to believe in Jesus. Likewise, many today claim to follow him. But who do they think Jesus is?

Some say that Jesus was a great moral teacher. He was just a wise and virtuous man, they say. He wasn't the Son of God. In another view, held by Mormons, God the Father and Jesus are two separate divine beings who each have a body.[1] Jehovah's Witnesses have another view: Jesus was an angel who became human.[2]

Jesus first told the disciples that he would use them to build his church only after he had asked them a question. He asked them, "Who do you say that I am?":

> Now when Jesus came into the district of Caesarea Philippi, he asked his disciples, "Who do people say that the Son of Man is?" And they said, "Some say John the Baptist, others say Elijah, and others Jeremiah or one of the prophets." He said to them, "But who do you say that I am?" Simon Peter replied, "You are the Christ, the Son of the living God." (Matt. 16:13–16)

---

1 The Church of Jesus Christ of Latter-Day Saints, "What Mormons Believe about Jesus Christ," https://ca.churchofjesus-christ.org/what-mormons-believe-about-jesus-christ.

2 Watch Tower and Bible Tract Society of Pennsylvania, "Our Readers Ask . . . Is Jesus the Archangel Michael?" https://wol.jw.org/en/wol/d/r1/lp-e/2010250

Peter's answer, Jesus told the disciples, is the rock on which he would build his church: "And Jesus answered him, 'Blessed are you, Simon Bar-Jonah! For flesh and blood has not revealed this to you, but my Father who is in heaven. And I tell you, you are Peter, and on this rock I will build my church, and the gates of hell shall not prevail against it" (Matt. 16:17–18).

The church has withstood the forces of hell for 2,000 years. It has done so by standing on the rock: Peter's confession of Jesus's true identity. It's this same question, "Who do you say that I am?", that led to the Council of Nicaea. And the Nicene Creed gave the same answer Peter did: "You are the Christ, the Son of the living God."

We stand on that same rock. And that's why we need the Nicene Creed as much today as ever. It's the confession of faith that hell will never prevail against.

Questions for Reflection

1. Who wrote the Nicene Creed?

2. What was the main question that the Nicene Creed needed to address? Do you think that's an important question? Why or why not?

Read Matthew 28:16–20

What's a Heresy?

Before Jesus ascended to heaven, he entrusted the gospel—the good news about who he was and what he had done—to his apostles. He told them to "make disciples of all nations, baptizing them in the name of the Father and of the Son and of the Holy Spirit, teaching them to observe all that I have commanded you" (Matt. 28:19–20).

This task that Jesus gave to the church is often called the Great Commission. It has inspired generations of missionaries to risk their lives in distant places in order to tell people about Jesus. It inspires pastors around the world every Sunday, as they preach the message of Christ's death for sinners. It inspires biblical scholars who strive to make sure the church clearly understands God's word. It inspires Christians every day, as they remember that God is accomplishing his purpose through his people.

But what, exactly, were the apostles supposed to say about Jesus? What did Jesus want them to teach people?

Jesus called the apostles to plant churches, passing on the truth about Jesus and the gospel to others. Yet the apostles and those who received the apostles' teaching continued facing opposition. False teachers kept gaining followers and claiming they had the real truth about Jesus. This led to conflicts within the church. Just as false teachers led the Galatian church astray, even though it was planted by Paul himself, the early Christian churches dealt with false teachings—heresies—in their midst.

The Council of Nicaea met in AD 325 in order to deal with heresies in the church. These false beliefs threatened both the apostles' teaching and the unity of the church. These heresies didn't say, "Don't follow Jesus." They said, "Follow Jesus. Here's who he *really* was." They all offered a version of Jesus different than the Jesus the apostles preached.

If Jesus Is God, Does that Mean God Isn't One?

One version of Jesus that became popular claimed that God the Father adopted Jesus as his Son. At his baptism, Jesus *became* God, but he started out as a normal guy like you and me.[3] This third-century heresy became known as adoptionism or dynamic monarchianism.

Another early heresy claimed that there was no difference between God the Father and Jesus. In this teaching, the three persons of the Trinity—the Father, the Son, and the Holy Spirit—are the same. Rather than distinct persons, they're three different *modes* of the one God. In other words, sometimes God reveals himself as the Father, sometimes he reveals himself as the Son, and sometimes he reveals himself as the Holy Spirit. This heresy is called modalism.

Both adoptionism and modalism wanted to protect the idea that God is one. Either Jesus was a man adopted by God or he is the same as God the Father. God is one God rather than two or three gods.

It's true that God is one. That's how the Nicene Creed begins: "I believe in one God." The Bible clearly teaches this: "Hear, O Israel: The Lord our God, the Lord is one" (Deut. 6:4). But both adoptionism and modalism opposed the biblical teaching that God the Father, God the Son, and God the Holy Spirit are one God but distinct persons.

A similar heresy led to the Nicene Creed. This heresy, called subordinationism, also grew from a desire to emphasize God's oneness. Subordinationism taught that Jesus was subordinate to—less than—God the Father.

The most famous teacher of subordinationism was Arius. He was a leader of the church in Alexandria, Egypt, in the early third century. The Nicene Creed met for the specific purpose of responding to Arius's teaching. For this reason, the more common name for this teaching is Arianism.

Arius believed that Jesus was divine in some sense. He was higher than normal humans. But he was still lower than God the Father. Arius didn't believe that Jesus, as God's Son, was eternal. At some point, God the Son was created. Arius said, "There was once when the Son was not."[4] There was a time when God the Son didn't exist, he argued. Jesus is in the category of creature, and not the eternal Creator.

---

3 Jaroslav Pelikan, *The Christian Tradition: A History of the Development of Doctrine, Vol. 1: The Emergence of the Catholic Tradition (100–600)* (Chicago: University of Chicago Press, 1975), 175.

4 Henry Bettenson, ed., *Documents of the Christian Church*, 2nd ed. (New York: Oxford University Press, 1963), 40.

Arius attended the Council of Nicaea. In fact, so did his pastor, Alexander, who opposed Arius's teaching and excommunicated him a few years before the council.[5] Alexander believed that Arius had abandoned the biblical, apostolic teaching about Christ.

Defending the Faith Once Delivered to the Saints

In the decades leading up to the Council of Nicaea, people were saying all kinds of things about Jesus and people began to choose sides. These disagreements caused major conflicts in the church. For that reason, the Roman Emperor Constantine called for a meeting to settle the issues. Leaders from the churches throughout the empire met in a city called Nicaea—located in present-day Turkey—in the year 325. Like the Jerusalem Council in Acts 15, this gathering of church leaders tried to reach agreement on the Bible's teaching.

The final version of the Nicene Creed—the one we read in church today—was crafted at the Council of Constantinople in AD 381. The first version, produced by the Council of Nicaea, shares a lot in common with the final version. But, as you'll see, the first version specifically notes and condemns the beliefs of Arius. It condemns his specific statement that "there was once when he was not":

> We believe in one God, the Father Almighty, Maker of all things visible and invisible.
>
> And in one Lord Jesus Christ, the Son of God, begotten of the Father [the only-begotten; that is, of the essence of the Father, God of God], Light of Light, very God of very God, begotten, not made, being of one substance . . . with the Father; by whom all things were made [both in heaven and on earth]; who for us men, and for our salvation, came down and was incarnate and was made man; he suffered, and the third day he rose again, ascended into heaven; from thence he shall come to judge the quick and the dead.
>
> And in the Holy Ghost.
>
> [But those who say: 'There was a time when he was not;' and 'He was not before he was made;' and 'He was made out of nothing,' or 'He is of another substance' or 'essence,' or 'The Son of God is created,' or 'changeable,' or 'alterable'—they are condemned by the holy catholic and apostolic Church.][6]

According to the creed written by the Council of Nicaea, those who denied the equality of the Son of God with God the Father, who taught that Jesus was a created being, had no place in the church. They denied the apostolic teaching about Jesus. They weren't truly Christians because they didn't believe in the true Son of God.

The Great Commission that Jesus gave to his church requires that the church respond to heresies. That is what the Council of Nicaea did. False teachings threatened the church, so the church's leaders gathered to clarify and affirm the biblical teaching about Jesus. Teaching the truth requires that we confront heresies.

That's still a vital task of the church. Heresies have cropped up again and again throughout the church's history. Heresies surround us today—often even inside the church. So the church must respond to heresies with clear statements of the truth.

---

5 Khaled Anatolios, *Retrieving Nicaea: The Development and Meaning of Trinitarian Doctrine*, (Michigan: Baker Academic, 2011) 18.

6 Quoted in Phillip Schaff, *Creeds of Christendom Vol. I*, https://www.ccel.org/ccel/schaff/creeds1.iv.iii.html.

That's why the Nicene Creed remains a precious foundation for the church. It's not the Bible, but it faithfully summarizes the Bible's teaching. It tells us the truth about our Lord Jesus Christ. It expresses the rule of faith, the core teachings of the Christian faith. It tells us the good news about our God and what he has done to save us. This is the truth we're called to treasure in our hearts and confess with our mouths. It's the apostolic faith that the church is called to preach Sunday after Sunday until "the end of the age" (Matt. 28:20).

Questions for Reflection

1. What's a heresy? How do you think the church should respond to heresies?

2. What are the heresies described in this lesson? What truth did all these heresies want to protect? What truth did all these heresies deny?

Notes

19

"WHAT YOU HAVE HEARD FROM ME IN THE
PRESENCE OF MANY WITNESSES ENTRUST
TO FAITHFUL MEN, WHO WILL BE ABLE
TO TEACH OTHERS ALSO."

———————————————————

2 Timothy 2:2

Isn't the Bible *Enough?*

Read Colossians 3:16–23; 1 Corinthians 15:3–11; 2 Timothy 3:16; Hebrews 4:12–13

Why Do We Need Creeds?

The Council of Nicaea met in order to protect God's people. These church leaders needed to respond to false teachings that were leading Christians astray and creating conflict in the church. The document they created, the Nicene Creed, faithfully expresses the rule of faith, the summary of biblical teaching passed down by the apostles.

But you might still wonder, "Do we really need creeds?" We have God's word, the Bible. Most of us own a copy of the Bible and can read it anytime. If we come across false teachings, can't we just check the Scriptures to see what's true?

These kinds of questions lead many people to say, "I don't need a creed or a confession of faith. I have no creed but the Bible." In fact, people often think creeds are *un*biblical. They're human-made, right? Unlike the Bible, they can contain errors. And even if everything in the creed is biblical, doesn't the use of a creeds imply that the Bible is insufficient? How does something like the Nicene Creed fit with the belief that the Bible *alone* is all we need for salvation?

In short, isn't the Bible enough?

Creeds Protect the Church

The Bible alone is the inspired word of God. It contains no errors. And it's sufficient—it's all we need to hear from God. The church doesn't need any new revelations. In fact, the church *can't* reveal new revelations from God. If a pastor tells you he has some new truth directly from God, be on your guard (Rev. 22:18–19). Our trust is in the Bible alone. We need to be watchful so that we're not taken captive by human teachings that claim to be from God (Gal. 5:1–12; Col 3:16–23).

But trust in the Bible alone doesn't mean that creeds are unnecessary or unbiblical. Arius, in fact, was a Bible guy. He used biblical texts to argue that Jesus was created. Jesus, he said, was divine in some sense but lower than God the Father, and he claimed that the Bible taught these things.

So we can't assume someone is right just because he quotes the Bible. And you and I can't just assume that we always read the Bible correctly either. We may not always understand the context of a verse or its literary genre or its grammatical construction. We may not know the whole Bible well enough to understand how a passage relates to the rest of the Scripture.

Instead, the church usually comes to a right understanding of Scripture when the Holy Spirit illuminates the word as God's people read and study it *together*. Sometimes, someone like the Protestant Reformer Martin Luther may come along, someone who seems to be standing alone with his Bible against a wayward church. But that's not typical. That's not how the Holy Spirit usually works in his church. And even Luther wasn't all alone. He condemned the church of his day, but he stood on the shoulders of earlier theologians and creeds.

Written creeds and confessions are necessary, then, because they teach the church and keep it accountable. They don't—or at least shouldn't—add anything to Scripture. The Nicene Creed doesn't claim to reveal any new truths from God. Its entire purpose is to guard the truth by faithfully *interpreting* Scripture. It was written to help the church understand the *meaning* of Scripture. And the lasting creeds of the church have often been written in response to heretics like Arius who claimed to teach biblical doctrine.

The Bible itself talks about how it can be misunderstood and misused. When the Jewish leaders didn't acknowledge Jesus as the Messiah, he held them accountable to the Scriptures. They should have known who he was—if they had interpreted the Bible correctly. He said to them, "You search the Scriptures because you think that in them you have eternal life; and it is they that bear witness about me, yet you refuse to come to me that you may have life" (John 5:39–40).

The apostle Peter warned not against those who reject the Bible but against those who "twist" its meaning. Referring to the letters of the apostle Paul, Peter wrote, "There are some things in them that are hard to understand, which the ignorant and unstable twist to their own destruction, as they do the other Scriptures" (2 Pet. 3:16). It's not enough, then, to say we believe in the Bible alone. The Bible alone tells us everything we need to know for salvation. But we need to understand it. If we twist its meaning, we lose its message. We won't know who Jesus really is or what he's done.

That's why the Nicene Creed is precious. It gives the church time-tested guard rails. It's a useful way to teach new believers the core doctrines of the faith. But it also keeps *all* believers from veering off the path.

And that includes the church's leaders. As a pastor, I need to be held accountable. My church needs to know where I stand. The church needs to know I'm preaching the truth about Scripture and not twisting it. They need to know I'm teaching the doctrines of the apostles and not making things up on the fly. And if I'm straying from the truths in our creeds and confessions, they can call me out on it.

Creeds and confessions protect the church because almost everyone, it seems, says that they believe the Bible. Arius quoted Scripture. Mormons and Jehovah's Witnesses say they believe the Bible. But they don't teach the Bible's true meaning. They twist the Scriptures. If we know the Nicene Creed, we'll see why their heretical beliefs aren't the apostles' teaching.

Does the Bible Say Anything about Creeds?

Creeds—summaries of biblical faith—weren't just invented after the Bible was written. The Bible itself includes creedal statements. These biblical creeds are models for the church.

One of the most ancient creeds in Scripture is, "Hear, O Israel, the LORD our God, the Lord is one" (Deut. 6:4). This is a statement of faith. The apostle Paul also gives us creedal language: "I delivered to you as of first importance what I also received: that Christ died for our sins in accordance with the Scriptures, that He was buried, that he was raised on the third day in accordance with the Scriptures" (1 Cor. 15:3–4). This sounds a lot like the Nicene Creed. It's part of the rule of faith. Paul says, *This is what I received. This was handed down to me. Now I'm handing it off to you. We confess that Christ died and rose again from the dead.*

Paul also uses creedal language elsewhere. Writing to his young protégé Timothy, Paul said, "Great indeed, we confess, is the mystery of godliness." Then he wrote what was probably an ancient Christian creed or hymn about Jesus, the Christ: "He was manifested in the flesh, vindicated by the Spirit, seen by angels, proclaimed among the nations, believed on in the world, taken up in glory" (1 Tim. 3:16).

In both the Old and New Testaments, then, the people of God created the summary statements of faith in order to pass the faith on. They did this to teach the faith to those who needed to understand it and to defend the faith against those who were trying to twist it.

These examples of biblical creeds matter just as much for us today. We have the same call that the church has always had: to learn, teach, and defend the apostolic faith.

Questions for Reflection

1. What characteristics of the Bible make it unique? How are creeds related to God's revelation in Scripture?

2. Why do we need creeds? How might learning and studying the Nicene Creed help you and your church?

Read Ephesians 4:11–14; Proverbs 4:1–4; 1 Timothy 6:20–21

Why We're Suspicious of Creeds

Churches throughout most of Christian history have relied on written creeds. Summarizing a church's beliefs about biblical teaching makes it clear where they stand. This makes creeds useful in many ways. Among other things, it keeps pastors and church leaders accountable. Creeds serve as guardrails to keep Christians from finding any meaning they want in the Bible.

Yet Christians who believe in the authority of the Bible can be suspicious of creeds. Those who believe that the Bible alone is God's word want to keep any human document from being placed above Scripture. Creeds, properly used, *support* the supremacy of God's word, but the wariness of some Christians is understandable.

Devotion to God's word, though, isn't the only reason people resist the use of creeds. Some of us may feel that creeds threaten personal interpretations of Scripture that we hold dear. We don't *want to* think more carefully about what the Bible actually says. We don't want to be challenged by the broader tradition of the church—and maybe find out that we're wrong. We don't want to let go of beliefs or practices that we've always assumed were biblical.

We may also resist the use of creeds for other reasons. Modern culture trains most of us to see the world and ourselves in ways that make it hard to accept creeds. Some of our most basic modern assumptions and values are, in fact, anti-creedal.

Creeds in the Modern World

In the United States, most people have been shaped by what the historian Nathan O. Hatch calls "the democratization of American Christianity."[1] This "democratization" refers to the extraordinary changes in Christian belief and practice in the early years of the nation. Often, political and religious beliefs in the new democratic society went hand-in-hand.

Hatch summarizes this "democratic spirit" in the American church with three main points:

1. Many early American Christians placed their trust in ordinary people instead of ministers, theologians, or teachings inherited from the past. In a society based on human equality, people believed everyone had the right and ability to interpret the Christian faith for themselves.

2. This trust in ordinary people usually meant that individual spiritual experiences had more clout than careful study of the Scriptures. Many early Americans took "their deepest spiritual impulses at face value."[2] Since creeds come from thorough, painstaking efforts to read the Bible correctly, they had little authority for American Christians.

3. Outsider religious groups that promised to liberate people from authority became more popular than traditional churches. Ironically, the leaders of these movements often gained great authority for themselves by claiming to promote equality.[3]

Since the days of Martin Luther, Protestant Christians have believed that Christ alone is the ruler of the church.[4] And Protestants believe that Christ rules his church through the Bible alone. Pastors and other church leaders only have the authority to preach and teach what's in Scripture.

But the new democratic Christianity of the United States, which may sound like a belief in Christ alone and the Bible alone, often placed authority in ordinary people or popular leaders instead of in the Bible. It has led many people to trust their own intuitions, experiences, and interpretations without testing them.

According to Hatch, this democratic Christianity still shapes much of the American church. And another historian, Mark Noll, argues that this American form of Christianity has become the dominant form of Christianity around the world.[5]

For that reason, it can be good to examine ourselves. If our impulse is to reject creeds, we may be guided by cultural assumptions we haven't tested. We may want to dismiss the Nicene Creed not because we believe in the Bible alone but because we trust ourselves too much.

The Bible vs. Church Tradition?

Cultural beliefs that undermine the Nicene Creed don't only come from America. In the modern world—especially the last 200 years or so—people in many places have become more and more

---

1 Nathan O. Hatch, *The Democratization of American Christianity* (New Haven, CT: Yale University Press, 1989).

2 Hatch, *Democratization,* 10.

3 Hatch, *Democratization,* 9–11.

4 WCF 25.vi

5 Mark A. Noll, *The New Shape of World Christianity* (Downers Grove, IL: Intervarsity, 2009), 11–14.

suspicious of the past. The heartbeat of modern society is progress. We prize scientific break-throughs, economic development, and growing political liberty. God, through his common grace, has brought good through these things. But this focus on the future often makes us distrust tradition and the teachings of the past. It can lead us to think a document like the Nicene Creed must be out of date.

For Protestant Christians, this distrust of the past can also seem like the right way to think about our faith. Don't Protestants distinguish themselves from Roman Catholics by believing in the Bible instead of manmade church tradition?

The answer, according to Protestant historian Carl Trueman, is "No." The Protestant Reformation didn't simply set the Bible and church tradition in opposition. Trueman writes, "In fact, *tradition* is not the issue; it is how one defines that tradition, and how one understands the way it connects with Scripture, which are really the points at issue. Indeed, this was the crux of the Reformation, which was not so much a struggle between Scripture and tradition as between different types of traditions."[6]

What does it mean to say that the Reformation was a struggle "between different types of tradi-tions"? According to Trueman, the Protestant Reformer John Calvin believed that "Protestants had the true tradition; it was the Catholic Church that had moved away from the truth. The point was simple and well-made: the tradition that transmitted the correct understanding of Scripture from generation to generation belonged to the Protestants."[7]

In other words, Protestants appealed to tradition rather than rejecting it. They wanted to reform the church by restoring the true Christian tradition.

We're not the first Christians to read the Bible. We're part of a community that has been studying God's word for thousands of years. And while error has often crept into the church, the "true tradition" of the church has always survived. That tradition is the one that has passed "the correct understanding of Scripture from generation to generation." If we believe in the Bible alone, then this is the tradition to which we belong.

Embracing Those Who Have Finished the Race

For Christians, the past isn't full of dead people. Instead, Christians from the past are alive. At this moment, they're in the presence of Christ. The church through the ages is a living community. When we worship on Sunday, we aren't only in the presence of the believers we see around us. Instead, the Bible tells us:

> You have come to Mount Zion and to the city of the living God, the heavenly Jerusalem, and to the innumerable angels in festal gathering, and to the assembly of the firstborn who are enrolled in heaven, and to God, the judge of all, and to the spirits of the righteous made perfect, and to Jesus, the mediator of a new covenant, and to the sprinkled blood that speaks a better word than the blood of Abel. (Heb. 12:22–24)

The "city of the living God" includes those whose hands we can shake and whose voices we hear singing. But it also includes angels and "the spirits of the righteous made perfect"—those Christians who have gone before us. We don't *see* them now, but they're alive, in the presence of God, and they're members with us of the heavenly Jerusalem. We have communion with them even now.

---

6 Carl R. Trueman, *The Creedal Imperative* (Wheaton, IL: Crossway, 2012), 16.

7 Trueman, *The Creedal Imperative*, 16.

But they're also alive in another way. They're alive through what they wrote and passed on to us. And like Martin Luther, John Calvin, and other Protestant Reformers, we should look to their wisdom for guidance. They have passed on the "true tradition," based on the right understanding of Scripture. As those who, like the apostle Paul, have "finished the race" and "kept the faith" (2 Tim. 4:7), they have much to teach us.

That's why the Nicene Creed is so valuable. It's one of the most precious and foundational pieces of the Christian tradition. It doesn't compete with the Bible's authority but instead helps ensure that the church remains faithful to the true meaning of Scripture. We should treasure and learn from it *because* we trust in the Bible alone.

Questions for Reflection

1. Have you ever held a belief based on a misunderstanding of God's word? If so, how were you convinced of the Bible's true teaching about that topic? Was it a struggle for you to let go of what you had mistakenly believed to be true?

2. Do you think of yourself or your church as belonging to a tradition? If so, how would you characterize that tradition?

Read Deuteronomy 6:4–7; 2 Timothy 3:12–15

Why the Next Generation Needs the Nicene Creed

The biblical creedal statement, "Hear, O Israel: The Lord our God, the Lord is one" (Deut. 6:4), is followed by instructions. God tells his people what to *do* with this statement of faith. He says, through his prophet Moses, "And these words that I command you today shall be on your heart. You shall teach them diligently to your children, and shall talk of them when you sit in your house, and when you walk by the way, and when you lie down, and when you rise" (Deut. 6:6–7).

God told his people that his word must be in their hearts. They must treasure it and obey it. But they also must *talk* about it. They must speak about the teaching he has given them every day. And who, specifically, should they tell? Their children. God calls his people to confess their faith not only in their hearts but in order to teach the next generation.

This applies to us. And it's one of the main reasons to both study the Nicene Creed and then teach it to others—especially your children, if you have them, and new believers. Of course, we should help our children memorize verses of Scripture and read God's word for themselves. But they also need help understanding the whole scope of the Bible. They need summaries of the Bible's teachings that can keep them from error.

Protestant churches have created wonderful tools to help Christians teach the Christian faith to new believers and children. The Heidelberg Catechism and Westminster Shorter Catechism, for example, are time-tested documents that use questions and answers to teach a basic but thorough overview of Christian doctrine. Christian parents would be wise to use one of these catechisms to teach the Bible to their children.

But the foundation of these catechisms, in many ways, is the Nicene Creed. Knowing and teaching the Nicene Creed, which most people can memorize in a day or two, is one of the more powerful ways we can obey God's call to pass on the faith to another generation.

The Calling of God's New Covenant People

This call to pass on the faith doesn't just show up in the Old Testament book of Deuteronomy. Many places in the New Testament talk about passing on the faith. The foundation, of course, is the Great Commission, Christ's call to the apostles to "make disciples of all nations" (Matt. 28:19).

One New Testament book focused on passing on the faith is 2 Timothy. In that letter, the apostle Paul urged Timothy to "continue in what you have learned and have firmly believed, knowing from whom you learned it and how from childhood you have been acquainted with the sacred writings, which are able to make you wise for salvation through faith in Christ Jesus" (2 Tim. 3:14–15).

Timothy had learned and believed the Christian faith as a child. Earlier in the letter, Paul refers to the faith of Timothy's mother and grandmother (2 Tim. 1:5). Paul called Timothy to hold onto the faith these women passed on to him, so that he could pass it on to others.

Paul's instruction to "continue in what you have learned" addressed persecution. Timothy, like all Christians, will be opposed by "evil people and impostors" (2 Tim. 3:13). By holding onto the biblical teachings he received as a child, Timothy would preserve the faith for himself and others when faced with those who want to destroy it.

In the same letter, Paul said, "By the Holy Spirit who dwells within us, guard that good deposit entrusted to you" (2 Tim. 1:14). This "good deposit" is the rule of faith, the pure Christian teachings that Christ gave to the apostles and that they gave to the churches.

Paul then told Timothy, "What you have heard from me in the presence of many witnesses entrust to faithful men, who will be able to teach others also" (2 Tim. 2:2). God called Timothy to be a pastor, a minister of God's word. He was receiving the apostolic mantle—not to add to the apostolic teaching but to faithfully pass it on to other teachers. Those other teachers, the next link in the chain, would then be able to teach still more Christians.

Pastors and elders have a unique calling from God to preach the gospel. But all of us have a role in guarding the good deposit and passing it on. And answering that call begins with knowing the rule of faith taught in the Nicene Creed.

Our Task: Passing the Baton to the Next Generation

Have you ever run in a relay race? In a relay race, one racer holds a baton in his hand and, when he's finished his lap, passes the baton to the next runner. Then that racer takes the baton and runs. When he's done, he passes the baton to the next runner. That keeps going until the race is over.

The Bible calls the Christian life a race (Heb. 12:1). From one angle, it's like a relay race. We're handed the baton of the apostolic faith, summarized in things like the Nicene Creed, and then we pass the baton on to others. We're called to hold fast to that apostolic faith, to run with that faith and cling to it. If you're a Christian, the baton has been passed to you. You don't want to drop it. It has been handed on from person to person for the last 2000 years. We need to hold onto it and pass it on to the church's next generation.

Yet many today have dropped the baton. We don't understand some of the basic doctrines of our faith. We don't understand the doctrine of God, the doctrine of the Trinity, or the doctrine of the Incarnation. These are foundational beliefs that the Nicene Creed teaches clearly.

One of my goals in this study is to help you pick up the baton. I want to help you take the faith once for all delivered to the saints and run with it. I want you to be blessed by this precious statement of faith, and I want to use it to bless those around you.

So that's our goal in the rest of this study. We're going to take a close look at this ancient creed, so we can "contend for the faith that was once for all delivered to the saints" (Jude 3).

Questions for Reflection

1. What are some verses of Scripture that call the church to pass on the faith? How does it say we should do this? How might the Nicene Creed help the church fulfill this calling?

2. How have you or your church tried to pass on the faith to the next generation? Do you think some tools and methods are better than others? Studying or memorizing individual passages of the Bible is vital, but what problems might we face if that's the only way to try to pass on the Christian faith?

Notes

"HEAR, O ISRAEL: THE LORD OUR GOD,

THE LORD IS ONE."

Deuteronomy 6:4

Who *Is* God?

Read Deuteronomy 6:4; Colossians 1:16

Do Christians Believe in One God or Three?

Not long ago, one of my children asked a question during dinner: "Dad, how can God be in you and in my brother and in mom, and still be one God?"

The Bible teaches that God is one. Deuteronomy 6:4, an ancient creed of the people of God, proclaims, "Hear, O Israel: the LORD our God, the Lord is the one." Christianity is a monotheistic faith. Christians believe in one God, and not many gods. That's what the Bible teaches.

And that's how the Nicene Creed begins: "I believe in one God."

But belief in one God raises questions like the one my child asked. If God is one, how can he be in you and me and every Christian all at once? If God is one, how can he listen to the prayers of millions of people at the same time?

Christians face a unique question: If God is one, how can he also be three? How can the one God be Father, Son, and Holy Spirit?

The whole Nicene Creed answers that question, but the creed begins with the oneness of God. What does it mean that God is one?

Are Christians Polytheists?

The first lesson of this study described some of the heresies that led to the writing of the Nicene Creed. Several heresies in the early centuries of the church attacked the biblical teaching that God is one. They said that Jesus *wasn't* God—or at least that he wasn't equal with God the Father. Arius, whose teaching caused conflict in the church and led to the Council of Nicaea, believed that God is one and that Jesus was created.

The example of Arius shows us why the church needs creeds. Both Arius and his opponents believed that the Bible was the word of God. To resolve the crisis, the church needed to understand and announce the true meaning of the Bible, which teaches that God is both one and three. He is one God who is three persons. This the mystery of the Trinity.

Many opponents of the early church said that Christians were polytheists. Polytheists believe in many gods. For example, the ancient Greeks believed that Zeus, Athena, Poseidon, and Apollo were all gods. Since Christians believe in the Trinity, some said, that meant they believed in three gods. To the Jews, whose Scriptures Christians claimed as their own, this was blasphemy. Belief in one God was the essence of their faith (Deut. 6:4).

Many people in the ancient world were polytheists. But the apostle Paul made clear that this wasn't what the church believed: "For although there may be so-called gods in heaven or on earth—as indeed there are many 'gods' and many 'lords' yet for us there is one God, the Father, from whom are all things and for whom we exist, and one Lord, Jesus Christ, through whom are all things and through whom we exist" (1 Cor. 8:5–6). In this passage, Paul echoes the *Shema* of the Jews, "Hear, O Israel, the LORD our God, the Lord is the one" (Deut. 6:4).

Like all the apostles, and Jesus himself, Paul was a Jew. In fact, his family pedigree and education in Jewish religion were exceptional. He called himself "a Hebrew of Hebrews" (Phil. 3:5). He had persecuted the Christian church before Jesus revealed himself to Paul (Phil. 3:6). After he became a Christian, Paul went to synagogues throughout the Roman world trying to convince his fellow Jews that Jesus was the Christ that the Jewish Scriptures had prophesied.

So Paul knew as well as anyone how vital it was to believe that God is one. Yes, he said, people believe in many "so-called gods." But for Christians, there is only one.

The One True God

Paul said, "For us there is one God" (1 Cor. 8:6). But the words "for us" shouldn't make us think that Paul was a religious relativist. He didn't mean that God is one thing for Christians and something else for Buddhists and that all religions are equally true. Instead, Christians believe in the one God "from whom are all things and for whom we exist" (1 Cor. 8:6). Christians believe in the one true God who made everything for himself.

In another letter, Paul tells us that everyone knows that this one true God exists (Rom. 1:19–20). Yes, people believe in many "so-called gods." The world's religions have a vast array of different beliefs. But people have this variety of religious beliefs because they push the truth out of their minds. Paul says they "suppress the truth" (Rom. 1:18). This denial of the one true God leads to God's wrath (Rom. 1:18). He made us for himself, and our worship of other "gods" instead of him is the essence of our sin and rebellion.

But Christians can say that "for *us*" there is one God because we have "one Lord Jesus Christ, through whom are all things, and through whom we exist" (1 Cor. 8:6). God the Son, "through whom are all things" became a man, Jesus Christ, who is now our Lord by faith. The one true God, who is one and three, made us his own so that he could be our God. Therefore, he's "*for* us"—we're his—as well as "for *us*"—he is ours.

The true God is one God, and all who put their faith in Christ know him. Jesus said, "Whoever has seen me has seen the Father" (John 14:9).

Questions for Reflection

1. What is a polytheist? Why were the early Christians sometimes accused of polytheism?

2. Most Christians struggle at times to understand how God can be both one and three. Has believing in the Trinity ever been hard for you? If so, how did you find peace with this teaching?

Read Genesis 1:1; 2 Corinthians 4:6

What Did God Do?

Belief in one God is foundational to the Christian faith. The Nicene Creed begins with the confession that God is one.

The creed then asserts another essential belief: God is the Creator. The creed says, "I believe in one God, the Father Almighty, Maker of heaven and earth, and of all things visible and invisible."

The created world isn't part of God. The world doesn't flow out of him as an extension or emanation of God. Many people, both ancient and modern, have believed in some kind of ladder of being. God is at the top. Fleas are at the bottom. Everything else is somewhere in between. But everything shares God's nature to one degree or another. Sometimes this is a form of pantheism, which means that everything is God—there's no essential difference between God and creation. Sometimes the ladder of being is panentheism. Panentheism means that everything in the world is God, but God is still *more than* the world.

Christians, however, believe that God and the creation are essentially different. God is eternal and almighty. He didn't need to make anything; he freely created the world. But creation had a beginning. Every creature is dependent on God for its life.

And Christians, like Jews, believe that God created the world out of nothing. He didn't just pick up some stuff that was lying around and give it form. Instead, he spoke. His word created something where there had been nothing at all: "And God said, 'Let there be light,' and there was light" (Gen. 1:3).

Creation Out of Nothing

This is how the Bible opens: "In the beginning, God created the heavens and the earth" (Gen. 1:1). The first words of the Bible introduce God as the Creator.

The Nicene Creed mentions two things about God before affirming that he's the Creator. It says he is "the Father" and that he is almighty. Almighty means all-powerful or omnipotent. In other words, God can do anything. When he created the world, God didn't have any help. After all, nothing but God existed. God created the world out of nothing through his almighty power.

But what does it mean that God is "the Father"?

This refers to God's character as the Creator: "But now, O Lord, you are our Father; we are the clay, and you are our potter; we are all the work of your hand" (Isa. 64:8). As a man becomes a father by bringing new life into the world, so God's fatherhood reflects his bringing the world into existence.

But "the Father" also indicates that God the Creator is the Trinity. God is *eternally* the Father because he has eternally had a Son. The Creed focuses here on the creative work of the Father, but, by calling him Father, it points to the fact that he has a Son. The Son also took part in the work of creation, as the creed states later. By the Son, it says, "all things were made."

The Bible affirms the Son's work in creation: "For by him, all things were created, in heaven and on earth, visible and invisible, whether thrones or dominions or rulers or authorities, all things were created through him and for him" (Col. 1:16). God the Father made everything "through" Christ. He also made everything "for" Christ. Creation only finds its purpose, or end, in Christ.

As the eternal, free, almighty God—Father, Son, and Holy Spirit—God didn't have to make the world. You and I aren't necessary. God didn't have a man-shaped hole in his heart he needed to fill. He didn't think, "It'd be nice to have some company. I'm pretty lonely." No, God didn't create because he had any need.

Instead, God created the world out of love. He created the world to display his glory and share his glory with his creatures. It is part of our created natures, then, that you and I exist to glorify God and enjoy him forever (WSC 1). We're made to know him and love him. We're made for the glory of God. That's the purpose of our lives.

But what, exactly, did God create out of nothing? He made "heaven and earth" and "all things visible and invisible." He created everything we can see. But he also made the angels, the residents of heaven that we can't see. Even angels aren't divine. God made them in the beginning. God alone is eternal.

The God we glorify is the Maker of the heavens and the earth. The One True God made everything that exists.

The Creator Cares for His Creation

The Greek philosopher Aristotle believed in a creator. He called it "the prime mover." Basically, this creator started the ball rolling, but then left creation to take its course. Likewise, many Enlightenment thinkers, like Benjamin Franklin, were deists. They believed in a god who created the world and then left it to govern itself by natural laws.

But God didn't just create the world and then leave it alone. The Bible teaches that God cares for his creation in its smallest details. He sustains it every moment "by the word of his power" (Heb. 1:3). Jesus told his disciples, "But even the hairs of your head are all numbered" (Matt. 10:30). God knows every detail about you. He sustains your life every moment.

God the Creator remains present with his creation. He provides his creatures with everything they need. That's why this divine care is called providence.

We aren't polytheists; we believe in one God. We aren't pantheists; we don't believe that God is the same as his creation. He made everything that exists from nothing. But we're also not deists. We don't believe that God just leaves the world to do its own thing.

No, we believe in a God who created the world out of nothing and cares for it every moment. The Nicene Creed confesses a Creator who knows us and who cares for the intimate details of our lives with his almighty power.

Questions for Reflection

1. Why does the Nicene Creed call God "the Father"?

2. Why did God create you? How does knowing God's purpose for your life help you when you face daily problems and decisions?

Read Job 38; Hebrews 1:1–3

Is the Doctrine of God Practical?

The Nicene Creed teaches astounding things. Thinking about the eternal God and his attributes can blow our minds. These majestic truths draw our thoughts away from the daily issues that usually absorb our attention. The doctrine of God draws us to the heart of everything: the God who was, and is now, and ever shall be. You and I and our problems are so tiny in comparison: "What is your life? For you are a mist that appears for a little time and then vanishes" (James 4:14).

You're a mist. So am I. But God is forever.

Maybe, though, you're thinking that these majestic truths about God offer little help with your problems. Because the doctrine of God seems distant from everyday life, you may think it's not practical.

Of course, turning our thoughts away from our troubles and earthly desires can itself transform how we see our lives. But I want to show you a few ways that the doctrine of God can have extraordinary practical implications. God is majestic and eternal, but he also cares for his creation in every detail.

When God spoke to Job out of the whirlwind, he reminded him of this:

> Do you know when the mountain goat gives birth?
> Do you observe the calving of the does?
> Can you number the months that they fulfill, and do you know the time when they give birth, when they crouch, bring forth their offspring, and are delivered of their young?
> Their young ones become strong; they grow up in the open; they go out and do not return to them. (Job 39:1–4)

Job didn't understand why he was suffering and wanted to defend himself in God's courtroom.

God responded to him by talking about the natural world. He reminded Job that, as the Creator of everything, he tirelessly cares for his creatures. He attends to endless details that you and I and Job aren't even aware of.

Job was humbled by the awesome presence of God (Job 42:1–6). In the end, the knowledge of God's providence brings us comfort. We need to know that God is in control.

What Is God's Role in Your Life?

So, here are four practical takeaways from the doctrine of providence, written by the theologian Caspar Olevianus.[1] These are from his study of another early creed called the Apostles' Creed. Like the Nicene Creed, the Apostles' Creed affirms that God is the creator and, by his providence, the sustainer of everything.

1. **Every Christian can be certain that God watches us with the same almighty power by which God created everything.** The same God who made everything from nothing cares for us, provides for us, and governs our lives. God "upholds the universe by the word of his power" (Heb. 1:3). Jesus said, "Are not two sparrows sold for a penny? And not one of them will fall to the ground apart from your Father. But even the hairs on your head are all numbered. Fear not, therefore; you are of more value than many sparrows" (Matt. 10:29–31).

    Fear not. Not one sparrow falls to the ground apart from the will of Almighty God. Surely, he will care for you.

    The Nicene Creed reminds us of this enormously comforting truth. And coming face to face with God's providence leads us to worship.

2. **Everything happens for our *good*.** Everything that comes to pass in God's providence serves your salvation. As a pastor, it's hard to talk to people in my congregation who are hurting. The apostle Paul described horrible things we may face as Christians (Rom. 8:35). Many Christians have even been martyred for their faith, but he says, "I am sure that neither death nor life, nor angels nor rulers, nor things present nor things to come, nor powers, nor height nor depth, nor anything else in all creation, will be able to separate us from the love of God in Christ Jesus our Lord" (Rom. 8:38–9).

    In fact, Paul writes, "For those who love God all things work together for good, for those who are called according to his purpose" (Rom. 8:28).

    So, nothing can separate us from the love of Christ. And everything that does happen to us—*"all things"* that happen to us—works for our good. If we suffer because others have sinned against us, we know that God will punish these sins (Rom. 12:19). He is just. Even our suffering aids our salvation (Rom. 8:28–30; 2 Cor. 4:16–18). In the meantime, we can be certain that our suffering isn't meaningless.

    This should comfort us. The same God who made everything out of nothing can use even your pain for your good and salvation. We rest in the hands of the almighty God who knows every hair on our heads.

---

1 Casper Olevianus, *An Exposition of the Apostles' Creed* (Grand Rapids, MI: Reformation Heritage Books, 2020), 93–100. I've listed four of Olevianus's five takeaways here.

3. **The people around you are governed by God's providence.** You may turn on the news and say, "Boy, everything is just getting out of hand. Who's in control?" The Lord God Almighty, seated on his throne, says, "I'm still in control." God even rules the angels that we can't see. These spiritual beings are involved in our everyday lives in hidden ways (Heb. 1:14), but they're under God's control. The God who made all things governs all things.

4. **We should use the means that God offers.** Olevianus says, "Yes, God controls everything. But you and I are also called to use the means that God has given us to draw nearer to him." God has given means through which to know him and his grace.

   What are those means? Studying the word of God, prayer, and the sacraments (baptism and the Lord's Supper). These things saturate us with the gospel. They help us to fix our eyes on Jesus. They help us trust that God works all things for our good.

I hope you see how our doctrine of God can be a great comfort. By confessing who God is, it also implies how practical theology can be. If our God isn't the Father almighty, then he can't care perfectly for us, his children. But the Nicene Creed tells us that God is, in fact, our almighty heavenly Father.

The Nicene Creed summarizes, in just a sentence, the reality that God is on the throne. He spoke all things into existence and cares for his creatures. So we can have great hope, no matter what's happening in our lives.

Questions for Reflection

1. What are the four implications of God's providence that Caspar Olevianus described?

2. Do you find the doctrine of God's providence comforting? Why or why not?

"I AND THE FATHER ARE ONE."

_____

John 10:30

Who *Is* Jesus?

Read Matthew 16:13–20; John 4:39–42

Does It Matter Who Jesus Is?

After affirming that God is one, the Nicene Creed focuses on Jesus, the eternal Word of God. This section on Jesus is the longest part of the creed. It answers the most important question you'll ever ask in your life: "Who is Jesus?"

That question has eternal stakes. And it's a question that Jesus asked his disciples. People had been saying many different things about him. They weren't sure who he was. Even John the Baptist, whom God had sent to announce the coming of the Messiah, got confused. From prison, John sent Jesus this message: "Are you the one who is to come, or shall we look for another?" (Matt. 11:3).

So Jesus asked his disciples, "Who do you say that I am?" (Matt. 16:15).

Modern people often think we shouldn't worry too much about the answer to this question. As long as we love Jesus and obey his command to love other people, we're good. Debating religious doctrine is tacky. It's a waste of time. And how could we ever be sure of the truth anyway?

But Jesus didn't avoid this question. He asked his disciples, and he asks us, "Who do you say that I am?"

Who Did Jesus Say He Was?

When Jesus asked the disciples, "Who do you say that I am?" Peter answered, "You are the Christ, the Son of the living God." Peter got it right: "And Jesus answered him, 'Blessed are you, Simon bar Jonah! For flesh and blood has not revealed this to you, but my Father who is in heaven'" (Matt. 16:17).

As in the early church, people today have different ideas about Jesus. They say he was a great moral teacher, a prophet like Muhammad, a spiritual guide, a political revolutionary, or maybe just a phony religious guru. But Jesus doesn't give us the option of believing any of those things about him. It's only Peter's answer that Jesus blessed.

In the end, we can only affirm that Jesus is the Christ, the Son of the living God—or deny it.

In *Mere Christianity,* C. S. Lewis made an argument sometimes referred to as the "trilemma." He said there are three possible conclusions we could reach about Jesus:

> I am trying here to prevent anyone saying the really foolish thing that people often say about (Jesus): I'm ready to accept Jesus as a great moral teacher, but I don't accept his claim to be God. That is the one thing we must not say. A man who was merely a man and said the sort of things Jesus said would not be a great moral teacher. He would either be a lunatic—on the level with the man who says he is a poached egg—or else he would be the Devil of Hell. You must make your choice. Either this man was, and is, the Son of God, or else a madman or something worse. You can shut him up for a fool, you can spit at him and kill him as a demon or you can fall at his feet and call him Lord and God, but let us not come with any patronising nonsense about his being a great human teacher. He has not left that open to us. He did not intend to. . . . Now it seems to me obvious that He was neither a lunatic

nor a fiend: and consequently, however strange or terrifying or unlikely it may seem, I have to accept the view that He was and is God.[1]

I love what Lewis says here. He says, "Look, there are no other options, according to Jesus's own words." We can't embrace a Jesus who was just a great teacher or just a prophet. Jesus claimed to be far more than any of that. He is the eternal Son of the Father.

The Nicene Creed, too, identifies Jesus as the Son of God. It elaborates on Peter's answer, drawing on the full biblical testimony about Jesus. The Nicene Creed answers the question "Who is Jesus?" this way: "I believe in one Lord Jesus Christ, the only begotten Son of God, begotten of the Father before all worlds; God of God, Light of Light, very God of very God; begotten, not made, being of one substance with the Father, by whom all things were made."

Jesus is the Christ. He's the Son of God. That means he *is* God. The Lord Jesus Christ is "very God of very God."

Can't We Just Agree to Love Jesus?

Sometimes, well-meaning Christians say, "Can't we just agree to love Jesus and not nitpick about who exactly he was? We can all agree that Jesus was great, right? Can't we focus on doing what he said instead of debating who he was?"

But we see even from human relationships that we're limited in our love for people we don't know anything about. Yes, we can help strangers. We can offer them water, money, shelter, or a listening ear. You can help a stranger with her flat tire or perform CPR when the guy next to you at the ballpark collapses. You can share the gospel with someone you meet on an airplane.

These are all genuine acts of love.

But our love for strangers can never be like our love for our spouses, our children, or brothers and sisters in Christ whom we've known for years. As we learn about people, as we find out who they are, our affection for them and our ability to serve them grows. And the Bible uses these intimate relationships as pictures of the love between Christ and his church. We're his brothers and sisters (Rom. 8:29). We're his bride (Eph. 5:32).

How much can we really love Jesus if we're not sure who he is?

Clearly, Jesus wanted us to know his identity. Over and over again in the Gospels, Jesus tells people about himself. He said, "I am the good shepherd" (John 10:14), "I am the light of the world" (John 8:12), and "I am the living bread that came down from heaven" (John 6:51). He told people why he came: "For this purpose I have come into the world—to bear witness to the truth" (John 18:37).

He also said this: "I and the Father are one" (John 10:30). We know he spoke clearly about himself, since, as soon as he said it, "the Jews picked up stones again to stone him" (John 10:31). They knew that he had said he was God (John 10:33).

This is just a small sample of all that Jesus said about himself. He wanted to be known. He knew that we needed to know him.

Jesus asks you the same question he asked the disciples. It's the question he asks everyone: "Who do you say I am?"

---

1 C. S. Lewis, *Mere Christianity* (New York: HarperCollins Publishers, 2009), 55–56.

Questions for Reflection

1. What are 3–4 different ways that you have heard people you know answer the question, "Who is Jesus?"

2. What was Peter's answer to Jesus's question, "Who do you say that I am?" Do you agree with his answer? Why or why not?

Read John 1:1–14; 17:1–5

Did God Make Jesus?

The Council of Nicaea met in order to confront Arius's claim that God the Son, at some point, didn't exist. He was created. Arius claimed, "There was once when the Son was not."

But if the Nicene Creed rejected Arius's teaching, why does it call Jesus "the only begotten Son of God"? If he was begotten, doesn't that mean he was born? *Beget* means to father a child.

The creed uses the word "begotten" three times in this short section. It seems to be a big deal:

> And in one Lord Jesus Christ, the only begotten Son of God,
> begotten of the Father before all worlds;
> God of God, Light of Light, very God of very God;
> begotten, not made, being of one substance with the Father.

Why does the Nicene Creed choose this word, *begotten*, to prove that the Son of God was *never* born? How does the creed prove that the Son is eternal?

How Was Jesus "Begotten" By the Father?

You may not be familiar with the word *begotten*. The word likely comes from the writings of the apostle John. John referred to Jesus several times using the Greek word that means "only begotten" (John 1:14, 18; 1 John 4:9). Building on this biblical precedent, many ancient theologians also referred to Jesus as "the only begotten."

So this is an important term. It's a biblical term. But what exactly does it mean?

First of all, the creed contrasts "begotten" with the word "made." The Son of God was "begotten, not made." This is huge. The Son of God was not created. He wasn't made. Therefore, he has always existed. So, whatever "begotten" means, we know already that it doesn't mean that at some point God the Son was born.

In the incarnation, of course, the Son of God was born as a man (Luke 2:30–35), Jesus Christ. Jesus was both true God and true man. As a man, he *was* born at a particular time in human history to a young Jewish woman. But that's not what the creed is talking about here—it's not referring to his human origins, but to his *divine* origins. It's saying, against Arius, that God the Son always existed. He was never born nor made.

So, if the Son of God is eternal, does that mean he *is* God? Couldn't he be another, separate eternal being?

No, the creed has already affirmed the biblical belief in one God who created all things. This section on Jesus builds on the confession that God is one. If God is one and everything else was created, then no other eternal beings exist. If the Son of God is eternal, then he's God. There are no other options.

But the creed also says this directly: the Lord Jesus Christ is "one substance with the Father." The Son of God was never made. He's eternal. And he shares the same "substance" with God the Father. He's not another being. The Father and the Son are one God.

What, then, does the word "begotten" tell us? It tells us about the eternal relationship between God the Father and God the Son. It's a biblical term that helps us understand the relationship among the persons of the Trinity who have always existed. God the Father is eternally unbegotten. The Son is eternally begotten of the Father. The Holy Spirit, as we'll see, "proceeds from the Father and the Son." Yes, the Son comes from the Father, but not as a creature coming into existence. There was never a time when this Trinitarian relationship didn't exist.

The persons of the Trinity—Father, Son, and Holy Spirit—are equal in power and glory. But they're distinct from one another. The Nicene Creed's use of *begotten*, therefore, refutes modalism as well as Arianism. The modalist heresy taught that the Father, the Son, and the Holy Spirit were *modes* of God. The one God just revealed himself in different ways at different times. But that isn't the Bible's teaching (John 16:12–15), as the creed makes clear.

The rest of this part of the creed likely seems more straightforward. Jesus is "God of God" and "very God of very God." This language is strong and clear. It's hard to miss the point: Jesus is God.

Has Arius Ever Knocked on Your Door?

You know who else teaches what Arius taught, that Jesus was just a creature?

Actually, a lot of people share Arius's beliefs about Jesus. But the ones you've most likely come across are Jehovah's Witnesses. Many of us have heard them knock on our doors. Maybe you hide behind the couch when they come. Maybe you go to the door and tell them to go away. But if you've ever talked with them or looked at their booklets, you'll see they make the same arguments that Arius made long ago.

Jehovah's Witnesses say that Jesus is a creature. They point to verses in the Bible like Colossians 1:15–16, "He is the image of the invisible God, the firstborn of all creation. For by him all things were created, in heaven and on earth, visible and invisible, whether thrones or dominions, rulers or authorities—all things were created through him and for him." Jehovah's Witnesses say, "See, he's the firstborn of creation. He's the first thing God created."

So did the Nicene Creed get this wrong?

No. First of all, this verse needs to be interpreted in the context of other verses which refer to Jesus as God (John 1:1–14, 10:30).

But, second, what does Colossians 1:15 actually mean by referring to Jesus as "the firstborn of all creation"? We can answer this by looking to the Old Testament. What did it mean in Israel to be the firstborn?

Being the firstborn meant being preeminent. In Psalm 89:27, God speaks about David or a Davidic King as "the firstborn": "I will make him the firstborn, the highest of the kings of the earth." But David wasn't the firstborn in his family. He had many older brothers. By calling him the firstborn, God says, "I will *make* him the firstborn. He's going to be over all others."

That's what Paul means in Colossians 1:15. Jesus, who made all things, is the preeminent one, the all-glorious one. He was eternally begotten, but not made. He was never born.

Ancient heresies twisted the words of Scripture so that people would believe a lie. And people today twist the Scriptures, too. That's why we need to understand Bible verses in context. That's why we need to understand the full witness of Scripture.

And that's why we need the Nicene Creed. The creed keeps us from errors like this. It keeps us from looking at a biblical verse outside of its biblical and historical context and twisting its meaning. The creed tells us, summing up the apostolic witness of Scripture, that Jesus Christ is "God of God, Light of Light, very God of God."

Questions for Reflection

1. What does the Nicene Creed mean when it says that Jesus is "begotten"?

2. Sometimes people say that the Trinity is just a complicated mystery that has no practical purpose. For that reason, it's not something Christians should bother thinking about too much. Do you think that's true? Why or why not?

Read John 1:4–9; 1 Timothy 6:13–16; 1 John 1:5

The Glory of the Trinity

The Nicene Creed teaches that Jesus is God. By using the biblical term "begotten," it shows that Jesus is one with the Father and yet a distinct person. God the Son is eternally begotten of the Father. He wasn't made. There was never a time when he didn't exist.

In this way, the creed condemned both Arius and modalism. Against Arius, it said that Jesus was the eternal Son of God. Against modalism, the creed said that God the Son was a distinct person. As the "only begotten," he has an eternal relationship with God the Father. In this way, the Nicene Creed provided language for talking about the Holy Trinity that has guided the church for over 1,500 years. It's a precious and clear expression of the biblical doctrine of God.

But the creed also gives us another image to help us understand who Jesus is. Jesus is "Light of Light." What does this mean? Why is it in the creed?

Like "begotten," "light" is a term the Bible uses to describe Jesus. Jesus said, "I am the light of the world" (John 8:12). Light suggests purity. It suggests knowledge. As the light of the world, Jesus makes God and his salvation known.

Light also refers to glory: "We have seen his glory, glory as of the only Son from the Father" (John 1:14). As the light of the world, Jesus reveals the glory of the Father.

Fire and Light

The Bible teaches that Jesus is "Light of Light." He is "the radiance of the glory of God, and the exact imprint of his nature" (Heb. 1:3). When people see Jesus, they see the glory of the Father (John 14:9; 17:4).

You can't separate light from a fire. Likewise, you can't separate the Son, who is light, from the Father.

This is how John of Damascus, an ancient theologian, explained this image of light:

> Just as the light has ever been begotten of the fire, and is always in it, and is in no way separated from it, so also is the son begotten of the Father without in any way being separated from him, but always existing in him. However, the light which is inseparably begotten of the fire and always remains in it does not have any individual existence apart from the fire because it is a natural quality of the fire. On the other hand, the only begotten Son of God who was inseparably and indivisibly begotten of the Father and abides in Him always does have his own individual existence apart from that of the Father. St. Augustine wonders therefore, if he is sent not because he is unequal with the Father, but because he is a pure emanation, issuing from the glory of the Almighty God for there that which issues and that from which it issues is of one and the same substance. For it does not issue as water issues from an aperture of the earth or of stone, but as light issues from light.[2]

---

2 St. John of Damascus, *Writings: The Fount of Knowledge—The Philosophical Chapters, on Heresies, the Orthodox Faith*, trans Frederic H. Chase Jr. (Washington, D.C.: Catholic University of America Press, 2012).

Jesus is the radiance of the Father. As long as a fire burns, it gives off light. Neither the fire nor the light ever exists on its own. Yet they're distinct. In a similar way, the Father and the Son are one substance, yet distinct.

Will We Honor the Son?

Jesus wasn't just a good teacher. He didn't just have some nice moral lessons for us. The ancient Christian faith, the faith once-for-all delivered to the saints, tells us that Jesus is Light from Light, eternally begotten of the Father, equal with the Father in power and glory.

This is what Jesus himself taught. We can't deny the deity of Christ without denying the teaching of Jesus. Jesus said, "For the Father judges no one, but has given all judgment to the Son, that all may honor the Son, just as they honor the Father. Whoever does not honor the Son does not honor the Father who sent him" (John 5:22–23).

The Nicene Creed draws from many different places in the Scriptures to answer the question, "Who is Jesus?" Those who wrote the creed, and those who later defended it against ongoing Arian attacks, were great men and women of the faith who held fast to the Bible. They wanted to pass the baton. They wanted to make sure that the next generation knew who Jesus was.

So who is Jesus? He's Light of Light. He's very God of very God. He's the Son of God, eternally begotten of the Father.

Questions for Reflection

1. How does the phrase "Light of Light" help us understand who Jesus is?

2. How do you think we should honor God the Son? How does the image of "Light of Light" help us understand the honor he deserves?

"BY THIS YOU KNOW THE SPIRIT OF GOD:

EVERY SPIRIT THAT CONFESSES THAT

JESUS CHRIST HAS COME IN THE FLESH

IS FROM GOD."

---

1 John 4:2

How Did *God Become* a Man?

Read John 1:14–18; Philippians 2:5–11

He Came for Us

The Nicene Creed confesses that Christ is "God of God, Light of Light, very God of very God; begotten, not made." He is equal with the Father, and yet he's a distinct person. He's the radiance of the Father's glory (Heb. 1:3).

The identity of Jesus is essential to the Christian faith. The God we worship is one God. And the Son is God.

But this section of the creed isn't *only* teaching about God the Son's eternal nature. The Son of God is the "one Lord Jesus Christ." He's the Christ, the Messiah of Israel. And he has a first-century Jewish name—Jesus. If we *only* knew that the Son was the eternal radiance of the Father, we'd be in desperate trouble. As sinners, we're not at peace with this holy and glorious God. But the creed teaches that the Son became a human being.

The Jesus we know as our Lord and Savior was born to a Jewish family during the time of the Roman empire. And Mary and Joseph didn't pick the name Jesus from their baby-name book. The name came from heaven. The angel Gabriel said, "You shall call his name Jesus, for he will save his people from their sins" (Matt. 1:23). That's how *we* know God the Son: as Jesus, our Savior.

So who is Jesus? He's the eternal Son of God who became a man to save us from our sins.

The Light of Light Descended

One of my favorite times of the year is Christmas. I love meditating on the fact that God sent his Son into the world, that "the Word became flesh and dwelt among us" (John 1:14). I love the Christmas hymns that we sing about how God the Son came to save us.

In fact, our church sings one Christmas hymn throughout the year because we love it so much. It's called "Let all mortal flesh keep silence." It captures beautifully what we see in this section of the Nicene Creed. In verse 3 of this hymn, the "Light of Light" comes to earth:

> Rank on rank the host of heaven
> spreads its vanguard on the way,
> as the Light of light descendeth
> from the realms of endless day,
> that the pow'rs of hell may vanish
> as the darkness clears away.

The "God of God, Light of Light, very God of very God" came down from his home in "the realms of endless day." That's a picture of the incarnation of our "one Lord Jesus Christ."

So we're at a transition point in the Nicene Creed. We move from heaven to earth, from eternity to time. The Light of Light descended—he came down—and took flesh from the womb of the Virgin Mary. That's the mystery of the incarnation.

God became a man.

The creed says:

> Who, for us men, and for our salvation,
> came down from heaven
> and was incarnate by the Holy Spirit of the virgin Mary,
> and was made man.

The Humiliation of God

God the Son eternally radiates the glory of God. But becoming a man wasn't glorious. We often talk about his incarnation, life, and death as Christ's humiliation. When the Light of Light descended, it wasn't just a change in location. By becoming man, the Son of God set aside his infinite glory to become a creature.

The apostle Paul used this descent of Jesus as a model for the Christian life. Christian humility comes from imitating the humiliation of God the Son:

> Do nothing from selfish ambition or conceit, but in humility count others more significant than yourselves. Let each of you look not only to his own interests, but also to the interests of others. Have this mind among yourselves, which is yours in Christ Jesus, who, though he was in the form of God, did not count equality with God a thing to be grasped, but emptied himself, by taking the form of a servant, being born in the likeness of men. (Phil. 2:3–7)

Jesus, who is equal with God, became a human who would suffer and die. The almighty God, the maker of heaven and earth, became a servant. And not only did he become human, he was poor. When he was born, his parents put him in a manger—a box used for animal feed (Luke 2:7).

So why did he come down? Why did the Son of God humble himself? Why did God leave heaven? Did he descend just to give us a model of virtue? Did he only want to show us what humility looks like?

No, God came down to save us. Jesus Christ's humiliation reconciled us to God. Through his humiliation, he became the perfect human servant that God the Father desired. He became the one who could take our place on the cross and satisfy God's justice against our sin. And on the cross, he suffered and died not just as a man but as if he were a sinner, a criminal. At the cross, his humiliation reached infinite depths.

But through his humiliation, Jesus glorified God. After the shepherds went to see Jesus in the manger, they "returned, glorifying and praising God for all they had heard and seen, as it had been told them" (Luke 2:20). Because Jesus went to the cross, God the Father, "highly exalted him and bestowed on him the name that is above every name" (Phil. 2:9).

And through his humiliation, Jesus also glorifies *us*. When he prayed with his disciples the night before he died, he said to the Father, "The glory that you have given me I have given to them, that they may be one even as we are one" (John 17:22).

Jesus came to give us his glory—the glory we couldn't give ourselves.

The Almighty God of Love

The Son of God didn't have to come down for us. God is free. He could have left us in our sin. He could have said, "Go ahead. Do your thing. Keeping sinning. You'll get what you deserve." That would have been just.

But, instead, the God who speaks things into existence, the Almighty Father, sent his Son. Out of love alone, God became man. Jesus came clothed in human flesh to make sinners sons and daughters of God: "For God, who said, 'Let light shine out of darkness,' has shone in our hearts to give the light of the knowledge of the glory of God in the face of Jesus Christ" (2 Cor. 4:6). The Light of Light came down to shine his light in our hearts, so that we would know the glory of God—and glorify him as his children.

Questions for Reflection

1. Why is the topic of this lesson a transition point in the creed?

2. If you're a Christian, why do you think God saved you?

Read Matthew 1:16–22; Luke 1:26–38

What Is the Virgin Birth?

The incarnation, like the Trinity, is a mystery. We can talk about both based on what the Bible tells us. But there are limits to what we can say. We can't fully understand how Jesus can be both God and man. How could the eternal Son of God the Father take on human flesh?

While we don't know much, we know the incarnation happened through the power of the Holy Spirit. Here, when the Nicene Creed affirms the virgin birth of Jesus Christ, it mentions the Holy Spirit, the third member of the Trinity, for the first time. The Light of Light "came down from heaven and was incarnate by the Holy Spirit of the virgin Mary."

God is Father, Son, and Holy Spirit. And the incarnation is the work of all three persons of the Trinity. God the Father sent God the Son, and the Holy Spirit formed the Son in the womb of a teenage girl.

Our salvation, then, is the work of the Trinity. And that salvation began with the miracle of the virgin birth.

Is a Virgin Birth Possible?

When the angel Gabriel told Mary that she would give birth to the Son of God, she asked him, "How will this be, since I am a virgin?" (Luke 1:34). That's, of course, basically the question we all ask when we learn about the virgin birth: "How could that be?" How can a woman conceive a child without ever sleeping with a man?

Gabriel answered, "The Holy Spirit will come upon you, and the power of the Most High will overshadow you; therefore the child to be born will be called holy—the Son of God" (Luke 1:35). He tells her this birth will be a miraculous work of the Holy Spirit. The Holy Spirit will "overshadow" her.

The book of Exodus—the second book in the Bible—ends with God coming to be among his people. This scene includes the only use of Luke's word "overshadow" in the Greek translation of the Old Testament. It's used to refer to the cloud of glory, by which God had been present with them, settling on Israel's tent of meeting: "Then the cloud covered the tent of meeting, and the glory of the Lord filled the tabernacle. And Moses was not able to enter the tent of meeting because the cloud settled on it" (Exod. 40:34–5).

Luke probably expected his first readers to think of this scene. It was a momentous part of Israel's history. As God's presence had once settled on the tent of meeting, it now settled on Mary. God himself was going to take up residence in Mary's womb as he had once filled the tabernacle. God himself would take on flesh and become one with us. That's why Isaiah's prophecy about the virgin birth, which the Gospel of Matthew quotes, called Jesus "Immanuel," which means "God with us" (Isa. 7:14; Matt. 1:23).

We shouldn't assume, though, that everything the angel said made perfect sense to Mary. She didn't have a worked-out Trinitarian theology. She hadn't studied the Nicene Creed or even the New Testament, neither of which yet existed. She probably didn't fully know who the Son of God and Holy Spirit were, at least in their full Trinitarian senses. In all likelihood, we understand the incarnation far better than she did at that moment.

But here's what she did understand. The angel told her that Jesus would be "great and will be called the Son of the Most High. And the Lord God will give to him the throne of his father David, and he will reign over the house of Jacob forever, and of his kingdom there will be no end" (Luke 1:32–33). She understood that she would give birth to the son of David, the Messiah of Israel. The Christ. The king Israel had been awaiting for hundreds of years would be her child. She knew she had received the greatest privilege possible for a Jewish woman.

And she also understood this: the birth of her child would be a miraculous work of God.

But Are We God's Children, Too?

In order to save us, the Light of Light took on our humanity. He became one of us. In that way, he could be our perfect representative. He could live the perfect life that the first man, Adam, didn't live. Through Christ's holy life, the eternal son of God made those who trust in him children of God.

That's why God became incarnate in Mary's womb.

But is it a contradiction to say that we become children of God? If Jesus Christ is the only begotten Son of God, how can we also be God's children?

This isn't a contradiction. Jesus is the natural Son of God. By living and dying as one of us, fulfilling God's law in our place, he made us God's adopted sons and daughters. We're adopted only because we're united with Christ, the natural Son. Our adoption always, in every way, exists only in Christ.

And that's why we find the whole meaning of our lives in our hope of seeing the face of the Son: "Beloved, we are God's children now, and what we will be has not yet appeared; but we know that when he appears we shall be like him, because we shall see him as he is" (1 John 3:2).

Questions for Reflection

1. How is it possible for Christians to be called children of God if Jesus Christ is the only begotten Son of God?

2. How and when do you tend to think about the Holy Spirit?

Read Hebrews 4:14–16

How Can Jesus Be Both God and Man?

Once, I asked my Sunday school class, "Is Jesus a divine person or a human person?" Many of my students' eyebrows rose. Then someone said, "Well, Jesus is two people, right? He's a human person and a divine person."

What's the right answer? Is Jesus sometimes God and sometimes man? Is he *half* human and *half* God? Is he a divine person who just looks human?

The Nicene Creed confesses that Jesus is God. It also says that he "was made man." But how can he be both God and man at the same time?

The right answer is that Jesus Christ is one person with two natures. He's one person. But he has both a divine nature and a human nature. This answer comes from the Bible, and it was described in detail by the Council of Chalcedon, a gathering of the church that met in AD 451, more than a century after the Council of Nicaea.

There's no mystery more beautiful than this: Jesus Christ, our savior, is both the eternal Son of God and also, in every way except sin (Heb. 4:15), a human being like us. But, just as conflicts about

Jesus's divinity led to the Council of Nicaea, controversies about how these two natures coexist in Christ led to the Council of Chalcedon.

How Are Christ's Two Natures Related To Each Other?

The union of Jesus Christ's two natures is called the hypostatic union. The Council of Chalcedon gave us a definition of this union that has withstood the test of time. This, too, is a treasured creed of the church:

> Following, then, the Holy Fathers, we all unanimously teach that our Lord Jesus Christ is to us one and the same Son, the self-same perfect in Godhood, the self-same perfect in manhood; truly God and truly man; the self-same of a rational soul and body; co-essential with the Father according to the Godhead, the self-same co-essential with us according to the manhood; like us in all things, sin apart; before the ages begotten of the Father as to the Godhead, but in the last days, the self-same, for us and for our salvation (born) of Mary the Virgin Theotokos; as to the manhood, one and the same Christ, Son, Lord, only begotten; acknowledged in two natures unconfusedly, unchangeably, indivisibly, inseparably; the difference of the nature's being in no way removed because of the union, but rather the properties of each nature being preserved, and (both) concurring into one person and one hypostasis.

Several words in this definition may sound strange to you. For example, the Virgin Mary is called the *Theotokos*. This Greek word means "God-bearer." The word *theotokos* affirms that Jesus is one person by saying, "God was in Mary's womb." Can the infinite God who exists everywhere be confined to one woman's womb? No, of course not. But Jesus, who is both God and man, lived in her womb. So, as the mother of Jesus, Mary is the *theotokos*.

Therefore, *theotokos* helps us understand what this definition is saying about Jesus. He is "truly God and truly man." It wasn't his "human half" that was in Mary. Jesus, one person who is both "perfect in Godhood" and "perfect in manhood", lived in Mary's womb. His divine and human natures can't be separated or divided. These two natures also aren't mixed up together. And they don't change when they're united in the one person of Jesus. The two natures are "unconfusedly, unchangeably, indivisibly, inseparably" united in the "one and the same Christ, Son, Lord, only begotten."

That's who was in the womb of "Mary the Virgin Theotokos."

Some people had been saying that Christ's two natures basically existed separate from each other. They were called Nestorians. Others said that the divine nature more or less swallowed up the human nature, leaving Christ with one nature. They were called Monophysites.

But the Council of Chalcedon said, "No, those are both wrong." The natures of Christ are united. But they're also distinct. Jesus's divine nature didn't swallow up his human soul. Jesus was truly man not only because he had a human body but also because he had "a rational soul." He was human in every way, "like us in all things, sin apart." As truly man, Jesus is just like you and me—except that he never sinned.

Why Do We Need To Know About the Hypostatic Union?

But why does all this matter? Is any of it practical? Why do we need to know how Jesus's divine and human natures are related to each other? Why do we need to learn about the hypostatic union?

We need to think about the two natures of Jesus, first, because he is the Lord we worship. We want to know who Jesus is as well as we can so that we can love and worship him.

Second, the Chalcedonian definition is practical because it's only as true God and true man in one person that Jesus Christ could save us. He came "in the last days . . . for us and for our salvation." As true man, he could satisfy God's justice by dying for our sins. As true God, he had the power to overcome death. He rose from the grave so that we, too, can one day rise again.

The Bible tells us, "He was foreknown before the foundation of the world but was made manifest in the last times for the sake of you" (1 Pet. 1:20). The eternal Son became a man to save you. He took on flesh so that he could offer himself in your place.

The incarnation is still a great mystery. The Chalcedonian definition doesn't tell us everything about how Jesus can be both God and man. But it tells us enough to help us understand how Jesus could be our Savior. And it tells us enough that we might fall at his feet as our Lord, who is both God almighty and an intimate friend, who knows what it's like to be human.

He knows your joy, your pain, and your fears. He is Immanuel, "God with us."

Questions for Reflection

1. How would you sum up in one sentence the relationship between Jesus's human and divine natures?

2. Does thinking about the relationship between Jesus's two natures help you understand your salvation? Why or why not?

Notes

Notes

"FOR I DELIVERED TO YOU AS OF FIRST

IMPORTANCE WHAT I ALSO RECEIVED:

THAT CHRIST DIED FOR OUR SINS IN

ACCORDANCE WITH THE SCRIPTURES, THAT

HE WAS BURIED, THAT HE WAS RAISED

ON THE THIRD DAY IN ACCORDANCE WITH

THE SCRIPTURES."

---

1 Corinthians 15:3–4

What Did *Jesus* Do?

Read Exodus 20:1–2; Luke 1:1–4; 1 Corinthians 2:2

Jesus Was Crucified For Us

The Christian faith is based on historical claims. Yes, we serve an eternal and transcendent God. Yes, we meditate on his attributes and on the mystery of the Trinity. These magnificent realities are essential to our faith and lead us to worship.

But in a sense, these truths aren't really the foundation of our faith. They're not where we begin.

Unlike most other religions, Christianity doesn't focus on timeless truths or myths about the gods. Instead, Christians find their God closer to the ground. Our God has acted in miraculous ways, at specific times and in specific places, to save us and make himself known.

What did the apostle Paul say is "of first importance"? This: "That Christ died for our sins in accordance with the Scriptures, that he was buried, that he was raised on the third day in accordance with the Scriptures."

As Christians, the foundation of our faith is the incarnate Son of God, who lived on earth about 2,000 years ago. He was a Jewish man who lived in the Roman Empire. He had brothers and sisters (Matt. 13:55–56). His father was a carpenter (Matt. 13:55). He gathered disciples, announced the kingdom of God, and performed miracles in the Roman province of Judea.

And when he died, a particular Roman governor authorized his execution.

This next section of the Nicene Creed describes what the incarnate Christ did on earth, in history, to save us. It begins by telling us that the Lord Jesus Christ "was crucified also for us under Pontius Pilate."

The One They'd Been Waiting For

Throughout the Bible, God reveals himself to his people through his works of salvation. He fed them with bread from heaven in the desert (Exod. 16). He gave them victory in battles (Judg. 7:19–25; 2 Sam. 8). He saved them from executions (Dan. 3:8–30; 6:15–23).

But his most famous work of salvation was the Exodus. God's people had been slaves in Egypt. Then God heard their cries for help (Exod. 2:23–24). He remembered the covenant he had made with their forefather Abraham (Gen. 15:5–21; Exod. 2:24), and he saved his oppressed people. He sent plagues against Pharaoh and then made a path for his people through the Red Sea (Exod. 7–14).

Why did God save Israel in the Exodus? So they could know him. So he could be their God and they could be his people (Exod. 6:6–7). After saving them, he made a covenant with them (Exod. 19–20). This is called the Mosaic, or Sinai Covenant. The New Testament calls it the Old Covenant (2 Cor. 3:14; Heb. 8:6).

God had worked to save his people in the past. And in the centuries before the birth of Jesus, his people waited for another mighty work of salvation. They waited for the Messiah, who would bring Israel glory and freedom. He would restore Israel to the greatness it had known under King David and King Solomon. In fact, it would be even better.

Jesus was born in the midst of this history of God's works and God's promises. He came to do the greatest work of God. He came to fulfill all of God's promises (2 Cor. 1:20).

Like all firstborn Jewish boys, Jesus was taken as a baby to the temple in Jerusalem to be presented to God. When a faithful Jewish man in the temple named Simeon saw him, he knew that the wheels of history were turning. He saw the one he'd been waiting for his whole life (Luke 2:22–27). Simeon took Jesus in his arms and said:

> Lord, now you are letting your servant
>> depart in peace,
>> according to your word;
> for my eyes have seen your salvation
>> that you have prepared in the presence of all peoples,
> a light for the revelation to the Gentiles,
>> and for glory to your people Israel. (Luke 2:29–32)

Simeon had "seen the Lord's Christ" (Luke 2:26). Israel's great hope had come in the flesh.

Why Did Israel Reject the Messiah?

So, if Jesus was Israel's Messiah, why was he crucified?

Jesus Christ wasn't the Messiah most Jews wanted. They hadn't understood God's promises. They expected a military leader. They expected, at long last, to rule again in their own land—the Promised Land which God had given them after he saved them from Egypt. They expected a Messiah who would give Israel glory and safety again.

But that's not what Jesus did. And in the end, it was the leaders of God's people who urged the Roman governor to kill Jesus (Luke 20:20–25).

But the crucifixion didn't undermine God's plan. Instead, it fulfilled it.

At Pentecost, after Jesus ascended to heaven, the apostle Peter told a crowd of his fellow Jews, "Men of Israel, hear these words: Jesus of Nazareth, a man attested to you by God with mighty works and wonders and signs that God did through him in your midst, as you yourselves know—this Jesus, delivered up according to the definite plan and foreknowledge of God, you crucified and killed by the hands of lawless men" (Acts 2:22–23). Peter said that they, the covenant people of God, had turned over their Messiah to "lawless men."

But this happened "according to the definite plan and foreknowledge of God." And what was that plan? To save his people from their sins. Earthly glory and freedom would mean nothing if they remained under God's judgment. Instead of giving the people of Israel what they wanted, God offered them eternal life.

Peter told the same crowd, after they asked how they could be saved, "Repent and be baptized every one of you in the name of Jesus Christ for the forgiveness of sins, and you will receive the gift of the Holy Spirit" (Acts 2:38).

God planned the death of Israel's Messiah. He did this so he could forgive our sins and give us new life through his Holy Spirit.

The Perfect Plan of God

Jesus Christ came to be crucified under Pontius Pilate. And he came to be crucified "for us." He came to die in human history, as a man, in order to be the final sacrifice for our sins (Heb. 9:25–28).

Through the cross, we know the infinite love of God (John 3:16; Rom. 8:32). The crucifixion is God's great and eternal work of salvation. So don't put your faith in your feelings. Don't put your faith in whatever religious fads are trending right now. Put your faith in what the Nicene Creed tells us here.

The apostle Paul told the troubled church in Corinth, "I decided to know nothing among you except Jesus Christ and him crucified" (1 Cor. 2:2). That's the gospel. That's the event "of first importance." That's where we find the God of mercy and grace. So put your faith in this good news: the Son of God, the Light of Lights, became man to die for you.

Questions for Reflection

1. What does the apostle Paul say is "of first importance"?

2. In everyday life, what do you tend to think is "of first importance"? What's most often the top priority in your mind and heart?

Read 1 Corinthians 15:1–22

Jesus Rose from the Dead

When Paul reminded the Corinthian church of the things "of first importance," he didn't only talk about Christ's crucifixion. Paul said: "For I delivered to you as of first importance what I also received: that Christ died for our sins in accordance with the Scriptures, that he was buried, that he was raised on the third day in accordance with the Scriptures, and that he appeared to Cephas, then to the twelve" (1 Cor. 15:3–5).

This is what Paul calls "the gospel" (1 Cor. 15:1). It's the good news about what Jesus Christ did on earth to save us. After Jesus died, he was buried. Then, on the third day, the tomb was empty.

And that's what the Nicene Creed confesses. It uses Paul's wording almost exactly: "He suffered and was buried; and the third day he rose again, according to the Scriptures."

How important is this teaching that Jesus Christ rose from the dead? Well, here's what Paul said: "And if Christ has not been raised, your faith is futile and you are still in your sins" (1 Cor. 15:17).

In other words, if Christ's resurrection never happened, your faith is pointless. If Jesus didn't rise from the dead, don't bother being a Christian. If there's no resurrection, then Jesus's crucifixion didn't accomplish *anything*. It's just a miserable story. A crucifixion without a resurrection doesn't take away anyone's sins.

The Fact of the Resurrection

Paul said that Christian faith is meaningless without the resurrection. Then he said, "But in fact Christ has been raised from the dead" (1 Cor. 15:20). It's *a fact*: Christ is risen. The Nicene Creed confesses the church's trust in this fact on which eternity hangs.

Paul didn't use the word *fact* casually. As part of what he said is "of first importance," Paul listed the eyewitness testimony to the resurrection: "Then he appeared to Cephas, then to the twelve. Then he appeared to more than five hundred brothers at one time, most of whom are still alive, though some have fallen asleep. Then he appeared to James, then to all the apostles. Last of all, as to one untimely born, he appeared also to me" (1 Cor. 15:5–8).

Paul didn't say that Jesus rose in a spiritual sense in our hearts. He didn't say the resurrection was a symbol of this or that eternal truth. He didn't say that the resurrection is an inspiring idea that can motivate us to keep Jesus's teachings alive.

No, he said Jesus rose from the dead. The incarnate Son of God was dead and then became alive again and walked out of his tomb. The 20th-century writer John Updike described the resurrection this way:

> It was not as the flowers,
> Each soft spring recurrent;
> It was not as His Spirit in the mouths and fuddled eyes of the
> Eleven apostles;
> It was as His flesh; ours.
> The same hinged thumbs and toes
> The same valved heart
> That—pierced—died, withered, paused, and then regathered
> Out of enduring Might
> New strength to enclose.
> Let us not mock God with metaphor,
> Analogy, sidestepping, transcendence,
> Making of the event a parable, a sign painted in the faded
> Credulity of earlier ages:
> Let us walk through the door.[1]

The Christian church claims that Christ rose from the dead. That's the apostolic testimony. That's the Bible's teaching. That's the faith of the Nicene Creed. "Let us not mock God with metaphor," Updike wrote. The Christian gospel announces to the world: Jesus rose in the flesh.

---

1 John Updike, "Seven Stanzas at Easter" https://www.thegospelcoalition.org/blogs/justin-taylor/seven-stanzas-at-easter-john-updike/

And people saw him. Many people, actually. If they didn't believe Paul, who also saw the resurrected Christ, the Corinthians could ask one of the more than 500 other eyewitnesses, many of whom were still alive when Paul wrote (1 Cor. 15:6).

Eyewitness testimony is a key source of evidence in the courtroom. It's also, as Richard Bauckham points out, how *all* history is written.[2] To know what happened in the past, we read what people at the time *said* happened. Yes, we have to evaluate sources. But if we reject eyewitness testimony, we reject historical knowledge.

By appealing to eyewitnesses, Paul was saying, "Look, you have to believe this really happened. If it didn't, there's no gospel. There's no good news. So listen to the evidence. Listen to all these people who say they saw him alive after he died." Christian faith isn't believing something that goes against all factual knowledge. Facts are the foundation of Christian faith.

What's of first importance to Paul isn't a heart-warming symbol or inspiring story. It's a historical event. He reminded the Corinthians what happened and then told them why they should believe it.

Touching the Son

After the resurrection, Jesus made people face the fact that he was flesh and blood. He ate fish (Luke 24:42). Women clutched his feet (Matt. 28:9). When he came to a group of his disciples, he said, "Why are you troubled, and why do doubts arise in your hearts? See my hands and my feet, that it is I myself. Touch me, and see. For a spirit does not have flesh and bones as you see I have" (Luke 24:38–39).

When the apostle Thomas heard that Jesus had risen from the dead, he said, "Unless I see in his hands the mark of the nails, and place my finger into the mark of the nails, and place my hand into his side, I will never believe" (John 20:24). Eight days later, Jesus came to Thomas and told him, "Put your finger here, and see my hands; and put out your hand, and place it in my side. Do not disbelieve, but believe" (John 20:27).

The resurrected Christ showed himself to people. He told them to look at him, to touch him, to eat with him. They heard his audible voice. Jesus told Thomas to put his hand into his wounded side.

It's the incarnate Son of God raised in the flesh that makes God's salvation real for us. If Christ is risen, then our sins were truly paid for on the cross. If Christ is risen, then human flesh is now in heaven, glorified in God's presence. If Christ is risen, then he is alive and ruling all things. If Christ is risen, then we too will rise again and live forever.

What Kind of Body Does Jesus Have?

The end of Paul's first letter to the Corinthians is one of the longest passages on the resurrection in the Bible. Paul wrote to the Corinthians at such length about the resurrection because some of them had begun to doubt it (1 Cor. 15:12).

In response to this doubt, Paul closely linked Christ's resurrection with ours. If Christ rose from the dead, so will we. If he didn't rise from the dead, we won't either. And if there's no resurrection, "Let us eat and drink, for tomorrow we die" (1 Cor. 15:32).

---

2 Richard Bauckham, *Jesus and the Eyewitnesses* (Grand Rapids, MI: Eerdmans, 2006), 5.

"But in fact," Paul said, "Christ has been raised from the dead, the firstfruits of those who have fallen asleep" (1 Cor. 15:20). Christ rose from the dead first, but he won't be alone. Christians who have "fallen asleep"—died—will also rise again.

Then Paul addressed a possible objection: "But someone will ask, 'How are the dead raised? With what kind of body do they come?'" (1 Cor. 15:35).

He then answered this objection by saying the resurrection body will be different. Our earthly bodies are "a bare kernel," a seed planted in the ground (1 Cor. 15:37). But when we rise again, our bodies will be glorious, powerful, spiritual, imperishable (1 Cor. 15:42–44). We'll radiate God's glory in a finite way, with new bodies like Christ's: "Just as we have borne the image of the man of dust (Adam), we shall also bear the image of the man of heaven (Christ)" (1 Cor. 15:49). Our resurrection bodies will be flesh and blood, but they'll be glorious and new in ways we can't now imagine.

Our belief in Christ's resurrection is inseparable from this hope. If Christ is risen, we too will rise.

Questions for Reflection

1. How is the resurrection of Jesus related to his crucifixion?

2. Do you find the evidence for the resurrection persuasive? Why or why not?

Read Acts 1:1–11; Hebrews 10:11–14; Daniel 7:18

Jesus Went Up to Heaven

After Jesus rose from the dead, more than 500 people saw him. This included those who loved him most, like the apostles and Mary Magdalene. He wanted them to be certain he had risen. He wanted to give them hope. And he wanted them to be his witnesses "in Jerusalem and in all Judea and Samaria, and to the end of the earth" (Acts 1:8).

But he also told them that he wasn't going to stay with them. When Mary Magdalene saw him outside his empty tomb, he said, "Do not cling to me, for I have not yet ascended to the Father" (John 20:17). Many of these witnesses saw Jesus's last moments on earth: "And when he had said these things, as they were looking on, he was lifted up, and a cloud took him out of their sight" (Acts: 1:9). Jesus stayed on earth for 40 days after his resurrection (Acts 1:3) and then went up to heaven as his disciples watched.

The Rule of Faith, the core of Christian teaching, doesn't end with the resurrection. The Nicene Creed says that after Christ rose from the dead, he "ascended into heaven, and sits on the right hand of the Father; and he shall come again, with glory, to judge the living and the dead; whose kingdom shall have no end."

The ascension of Christ shouldn't be a theological afterthought. It's essential to our faith. Because Jesus has gone to Father, he now rules over everything as true God and true man. And after he ascended, he gave his witnesses "the promise of the Father" (Acts 1:4): the Holy Spirit. Through the Spirit, Christ formed his church and gave her power to "make disciples of all nations" (Matt. 28:19).

Through his Holy Spirit, Jesus Christ remains with his church today (Matt. 28:20). He rules, strengthens, and purifies her as he prepares her for his return (Eph. 5:25–32).

Jesus Went Up, the Spirit Came Down

The book of Acts tells the story of Jesus Christ's witnesses. It tells how they preached the gospel in Jerusalem, then in Judea and Samaria, and then across the Roman empire and to "the ends of the earth" (Acts 1:8). And this story begins with two extraordinary events: the ascension of Christ and the descent of the Holy Spirit at Pentecost. Acts 1 is about the ascension. Acts 2 is about Pentecost.

Basically, when Christ goes up, the Holy Spirit comes down.

Of course, the Holy Spirit has been key to the story all along. All of God's works involve all three person's of the Trinity. The Holy Spirit formed Jesus in Mary's womb (Luke 1:35). He descended as a dove at Jesus's baptism (Luke 3:21–22). He led Jesus to the desert to be tempted by Satan (Matt. 4:1). Jesus cast out demons through the power of the Holy Spirit (Matt. 12:28). And the Holy Spirit raised Jesus from the dead (Rom. 8:11).

In fact, the Spirit was so central to Christ's ministry on earth that Jesus said anyone who blasphemed the Holy Spirit would never be forgiven (Matt. 12:31–32).[3]

So the Holy Spirit doesn't become part of God's work of salvation for the first time at Pentecost. Instead, the church's baptism with the Spirit at Pentecost—when the disciples began speaking in different languages so that everyone could understand what they said—began a new era in the history of redemption. Christ had completed his work of salvation on earth; now, the Holy Spirit, through the church, would bring the message—and power—of that salvation to the world.

When Jesus ascended to heaven, he sent the Spirit. And through the Spirit, he's with his people "until the end of the age" (Matt. 28:20)

Jesus Sat Down

This is the last question the disciples asked Jesus before the ascension: "Lord, will you at this time restore the kingdom to Israel?" (Acts 1:6).

---

3 For an understanding of what it means to blaspheme the Holy Spirit, see https://www.corechristianity.com/resources/episodes/why-is-the-blasphemy-of-the-holy-spirit-unforgivable

These disciples believed in Jesus. They hadn't rejected him like the Jewish leaders. But they still seem to have had the same expectations as those who had turned against Jesus. They're wondering, "Will the Messiah now, finally, bring back Israel's glory and freedom?"

Jesus didn't really answer their question. But his ascension answered it. After the ascension, Christ began to rule as king. He "sits on the right hand of the Father," as the Nicene Creed says. The Messiah, the great Davidic king Israel had waited for, is enthroned—not in Jerusalem but in heaven. The Christ became king not only over the land that God had promised Abraham centuries earlier (Gen. 15:18–19). He became the king of everything:

> And being found in human form, he humbled himself by becoming obedient to the point of death, even death on a cross. Therefore God has highly exalted him and bestowed on him the name that is above every name, so that at the name of Jesus every knee should bow, in heaven and on earth and under the earth, and every tongue confess that Jesus Christ is Lord, to the glory of God the Father. (Phil. 2:8–11)

Jesus is the King of Kings. Because of his humiliation on the cross, he now has "the name that is above every name."

And as the king, Christ rules his church in a distinct way (Col. 1:18). He guards her from her enemies and sovereignly guides her.

But Jesus isn't just a king. He's a priest-king (Heb. 7). On earth, he offered himself as the final sacrifice for sin (Heb. 7:27). In heaven, in God the Father's holy presence, he prays for us, as the priests of Israel prayed for God's people (Heb. 9:24; Rom. 8:34).

So as God's people today, trusting in Christ and empowered by the Holy Spirit, we must live in obedience to the living, reigning Christ: "If then you have been raised with Christ, seek the things that are above, where Christ is, seated at the right hand of God" (Col. 3:1).

He Shall Come Again in Glory

As Christians, we look to the past. We remember that 2,000 years ago, Christ saved us through his death and resurrection. We also focus on the present. We "seek the things that are above," where Christ reigns now. The Holy Spirit now lives in us: purifying us, strengthening us, and sustaining us as we walk by faith in our Lord Jesus Christ.

But the Nicene Creed shows that the future is also key to our faith: "He shall come again, with glory, to judge the living and the dead; whose kingdom shall have no end." We believe that Jesus will come again. When he comes, our bodies will be resurrected, and suffering and evil will be no more. Christ's everlasting kingdom will become visible and fill all things. At that time, every knee will bow to Jesus, "in heaven and on earth and under the earth" (Phil. 2:10).

The angel who came to the disciples after the ascension said, "Men of Galilee, why do you stand looking into heaven? This Jesus, who was taken up from you into heaven, will come in the same way as you saw him go into heaven" (Act. 1:11).

Christ's kingdom, which already exists on earth in the church, will last forever. And God made this kingdom for us as well (Luke 12:32). Daniel prophesied about the coming of this kingdom 500 years before Christ was born: "But the saints of the most high shall receive the kingdom and possess the kingdom forever, forever, and ever" (Dan. 7:18).

Questions for Reflection

1. How are the ascension and Pentecost related?

2. What does it mean that Jesus sat down at the right hand of God? How might the knowledge that Jesus sits at God's right hand affect the way you think about your life today?

"GO THEREFORE AND MAKE DISCIPLES OF
ALL NATIONS, BAPTIZING THEM IN THE
NAME OF THE FATHER AND OF THE SON
AND OF THE HOLY SPIRIT."

Matthew 28:19

Who Is the Holy Spirit?

Read John 1:29–34; 3:3–8

Did the Council of Nicaea Make Up the Trinity?

The virgin birth was the work of the Holy Spirit, who "overshadowed" Mary (Luke 1:35). Just as he had once filled Israel's tabernacle (Exod. 40), the Holy Spirit formed Jesus Christ within Mary to be the Savior of the world. Then, the Holy Spirit empowered Jesus's life and ministry. And after Jesus ascended, the Holy Spirit came down to build and empower his church.

The Holy Spirit now becomes the focus in this next section of the Nicene Creed. Having confessed faith in the Father and the Son, the creed says that Christians also believe in the Holy Spirit, the third Person of the Trinity:

> I believe in the Holy Spirit, the Lord and Giver of Life;
> who proceeds from the Father and the Son;
> who with the Father and the Son together is worshipped and glorified;
> who spoke by the prophets.

With the Father and the Son, Christians worship the Holy Spirit as God.

But is that true? Is the Holy Spirit, like the Son, eternal? Is he the third person of the one almighty God? Is he equal to the Father in power, knowledge, love, holiness, justice, and every other divine characteristic? Should Christians worship the Spirit just as they worship the Father and the Son?

In short, is belief in the Trinity biblical?

Where Is the Trinity in the Bible?

The Nicene Creed's structure is Trinitarian. It begins by confessing faith in "one God, the Father Almighty." The creed then affirms that the Lord Jesus Christ is the eternal Son of God, equal with the Father: "God of God, Light of Light, very God of very God; begotten, not made, being of one substance with the Father." It then confesses faith in the saving work of the incarnate Son.

Now, it summarizes the church's teaching on the Holy Spirit.

But some people say that the Council of Nicaea made up the doctrine of the Trinity. For example, Jehovah's Witnesses say the Trinity wasn't taught in the early church. It was invented later. Earlier believers, they claim, didn't have this idea of Father, Son, and Holy Spirit.

When we look at Scripture, though, we see the language of Father, Son, and Holy Spirit all over the place. This Trinitarian structure in the creed comes directly from the Bible itself.

To show this, an obvious place to begin is with the Great Commission. When Jesus sent his disciples out to spread the gospel, he said, "Go therefore and make disciples of all nations, baptizing them in the name of the Father, and of the Son and of the Holy Spirit" (Matt. 28:19). The first Christians entered Christ's church through baptism, just like new Christians today. And how did Jesus say Christians must be baptized? In the name of the three persons of the Trinity.

The apostle Paul closed his second letter to the Corinthian church with this blessing: "The grace of the Lord Jesus Christ and the love of God and the fellowship of the Holy Spirit be with you all" (2

Cor. 13:14). In another letter, he wrote, "There is one body and one Spirit—just as you were called to the one hope that belongs to your call—one Lord, one faith, one baptism, one God and Father of all, who is over all and through all and in all" (Eph. 4:4–6). In both these examples, Paul named all three members of the Trinity together. He suggested their distinct roles in the life of the church, but also implies that they are one.

At Jesus's baptism, the presence of both the Father and the Holy Spirit confirmed that Jesus was the Son of God: "When Jesus had been baptized and was praying, the heavens were opened, and the Holy Spirit descended on him in bodily form, like a dove; and a voice came from heaven, 'You are my beloved Son; with you I am well pleased'" (Luke 3:21–22).

Further, John the Baptist emphasized the Holy Spirit's role in identifying Jesus: "I saw the Spirit descend from heaven like a dove, and it remained on him. I myself did not know him, but he who sent me to baptize with water said to me, 'He on whom you see the Spirit descend and remain, this is he who baptizes with the Holy Spirit.' And I have seen and have borne witness that this is the Son of God" (John 1:32–34).

The Holy Spirit came from heaven. He had the authority to identify Jesus as the Son of God. He appeared with the Son and accompanied the Father's voice.

Of course, the Bible also talks about the Holy Spirit at the very beginning. Before God had given any form to his creation, "The Spirit of God was hovering over the face of the waters" (Gen. 1:2). The Holy Spirit was with God at the beginning of time. The book of Genesis gives no indication that the Spirit was created.

Is the Holy Spirit Really a Divine Person?

So, the Bible often talks about the Father, the Son, and the Holy Spirit together. The Holy Spirit comes from heaven and existed before creation had form.

But does that really mean the Holy Spirit is God? Could he be an angel or some other created spiritual being?

If the Holy Spirit isn't God, why would Christians be baptized in his name, along with the Father and the Son? Why would Jesus, in the Great Commission, place the Holy Spirit alongside the Father and the Son, as though equal to them, if the Holy Spirit is a creature and not the Creator? God says, "I am the Lord; that is my name; my glory I give to no other" (Isa. 42:8). If God calls us to worship and glorify him alone, why would the Bible talk about a created being as seemingly equal to the Father and the Son?

Beyond that, it's the Holy Spirit who creates new life in a Christian. Jesus said, "Truly, truly, I say to you, unless one is born of water and the Spirit, he cannot enter the kingdom of God" (John 3:5). Without this new life, we can't believe the gospel. Just as the Spirit hovered over the waters at the first creation, he is the agent of the new creation in our hearts. Angels are messengers; the Bible never suggests that angels have this kind of power to create out of nothing.

From these verses, then, we can see why the early church saw the Trinity in the Bible. From the beginning, Christians were baptized into the name of the Father and the Son and the Holy Spirit. The doctrine of the Trinity wasn't invented at the Council of Nicaea.

Questions for Reflection

1. How did Jesus instruct his disciples to baptize people? How does that help us understand who the Holy Spirit is?

2. How do the pastors and members of your church talk about the Holy Spirit? What role does he play in the prayers and life of your church?

Read John 14:15–17; Acts 5:1–11

What Is the Holy Spirit Like?

The Nicene Creed confesses faith in the Holy Spirit as the third member of the Trinity. The creed affirms this faith in the Holy Spirit because some people at that time denied the divinity of the Spirit. They said, "Okay, yeah, I see that the Bible teaches that Jesus is God. But is the Holy Spirit God? Does he have the same substance as the Father and the Son? Is he equal with them in power and glory?"

Rather than the Trinity, they believed in one God in two persons: the Father and the Son.

But, as we've seen, the Bible affirms the Trinity. Christians are baptized into the name of the Father, the Son, and the Holy Spirit (Matt. 28:19). The Father, Son, and Holy Spirit are grouped together by the apostle Paul (Eph. 4:4–6; 2 Cor. 13:14). And the Bible teaches that the Holy Spirit is central to both the creation (Gen. 1:2) and the new creation—the new birth (John 3:5).

Studying the attributes, or characteristics, of the Holy Spirit gives us further evidence that he is God, the third person of the Trinity, "who with the Father and the Son together is worshipped and glorified."

Why Is He Called the *Holy* Spirit?

In the fourth century, the church father Athanasius said that some believed Jesus was God but denied the deity of the Holy Spirit. They had rejected Arius, who said that the Son was created, but they still only believed in two divine persons. He wrote, "Certain persons have forsaken the Arians on account of their blasphemy against the Son of God, and yet oppose the Holy Spirit, saying that he is not only a preacher, but actually one of the ministering spirits and differs from the angels only in degree."[1] These false teachers, or heretics, claimed that the Holy Spirit was equal to the angels and therefore a created being.

They based their argument on a Bible verse that says, "In the presence of God and of Christ Jesus and of the elect angels I charge you to keep these rules without prejudging, doing nothing from partiality" (1 Tim. 5:21). They said, "Look, Paul gives this charge in the presence of God and Christ Jesus and angels, but the Holy Spirit isn't mentioned. Maybe the Holy Spirit is one of the angels."

Athanasius responded to these heretics first by focusing on the attributes of the Holy Spirit. When the Bible describes the Holy Spirit, does he have the characteristics of a creature or of God?

It makes sense to begin, of course, with holiness. He is the *Holy* Spirit. That's what the Bible often calls him. King David said, "Take not your Holy Spirit from me" (Ps. 51:11). The prophet Isaiah said that when Israel was in the wilderness after the Exodus, they "rebelled and grieved his Holy Spirit" (Isa. 63:10). John the Baptist, speaking of Jesus, said, "He will baptize you with the Holy Spirit" (Matt. 3:11).

And Jesus called him the Holy Spirit when he promised to send the Spirit to his church: "But the Helper, the Holy Spirit, whom the Father will send you in my name, he will teach you all things and bring to your remembrance all that I have said to you" (John 14:26).

Holiness is an attribute of God. God is the Holy One of Israel (Isa. 43:3). The Spirit isn't *more* holy than the Father or the Son. They share in one holiness. But the Bible calls the Spirit the Holy Spirit because the Spirit makes *us* holy. He sanctifies us.

Even when speaking to a church struggling with many sins, Paul wrote, "You were washed, you were sanctified, you were justified in the name of the Lord Jesus Christ, and by the Spirit of our God," (1 Cor. 6:11). The Holy Spirit of God made this church holy. He set them apart as God's. In another letter, Paul said, "But we ought always to give thanks to God for you, brothers beloved by the Lord, because God chose you as the first fruits to be saved, through sanctification by the Spirit and belief in the truth" (2 Thess. 2:13).

Can angels make people holy? No, they're created beings. But the holiness of the Spirit shows that he is God. He doesn't just reflect God's holiness; he has the power to make holy those who have believed in the death and resurrection of Jesus Christ.

Does the Holy Spirit Have Other Divine Characteristics?

The Spirit is holy, but he's also sovereign. Like the Father and the Son, he is almighty, ruling all things. He is, according to the Nicene Creed, "the Lord and giver of life."

The Holy Spirit gave life in the creation (Gen. 1:2; Job 33:4). He also gives new life to sinners (John 3:5).

And we see that he is the sovereign Lord in a story in the book of Acts. When a married couple deceived the early church, the apostle Peter said, "Why has Satan filled your heart to lie to the Holy Spirit . . . You have not lied to man, but to God" (Acts 5:3–4). Lying to the Holy Spirit, in other words, is lying to God.

---

1 St. Athanasius, *To Serapion on the Holy Spirit* (CreateSpace Independent Publishing Platform, 2014), 1.

The Holy Spirit is also omnipresent (Ps. 139:7–10). He's omniscient—he knows all things (Isa. 40:13–14; 1 Cor. 2:10–11). He's all-powerful (Rom. 8:11–13).

In short, the Bible refers to the Holy Spirit as God. He is named alongside the Father and the Son. God's work of creation and salvation includes all three persons of the Trinity. And when the Bible describes the Holy Spirit, he has divine attributes.

The Nicene Creed confesses that the Holy Spirit is God because the Bible teaches that the Holy Spirit is God.

Questions for Reflection

1. Why is the Spirit called the *Holy* Spirit?

2. How does thinking about the Holy Spirit's divine attributes affect the way you think about his work in your life right now?

Read John 16:12–15

Is the Holy Spirit Distinct from the Father and the Son?

The Nicene Creed says that God the Son is "begotten" of the Father. This biblical term, *begotten*, describes the eternal relations of the Father and the Son. The creed also says that the Holy Spirit "proceeds from the Father and the Son." What does that mean?

Like *begotten*, *proceeds* is biblical language that gives us some idea of the relations among the Trinity. Jesus said, "But when the Helper comes, who I will send to you from the Father, the Spirit of truth, who proceeds from the Father, He will bear witness about me" (John 15:26). Jesus tells us that the Spirit "proceeds from the Father."

The Father is unbegotten. The Son is eternally begotten. The Spirit eternally proceeds from the Father and the Son. This is how the church talks about the Trinity. If God had never created anything, the one God would still have these relations among the persons of the Trinity.

But we also see a distinctive role of the Holy Spirit in God's work of salvation. He empowered the ministry of Jesus on earth. Now, the Spirit brings God's presence and power to his people, the church, as we wait for Jesus Christ to come again.

The Eternal Spirit

In his classic treatise on the Holy Spirit, Basil of Caesarea wrote, "The Holy Spirit is moreover said to be of God, not indeed in the sense of which all things are of God, but in the sense of proceeding out of God, not by generation, like the Son, but as the breath of his mouth."[2] This statement has a biblical basis. Both the Hebrew (Old Testament) and Greek (New Testament) words for *spirit* can also mean *wind* or *breath*.

The picture of breathing helps us see how the Holy Spirit can be one in substance with the Father and yet distinct. A human being must breathe. We can't survive without breath. If we're alive, we're breathing. If we're not breathing for more than a few minutes, we're—more or less, by definition—dead.

Likewise, the Spirit can eternally proceed from the Father without being created by the Father. The Spirit has always existed "as the breath of his mouth."

This gives us some sense of the relations within the Trinity. Yet at the same time the eternal life of the Trinity is really beyond our ability to comprehend. God is infinite; we're finite. God is eternal; we live in time. God is holy; we're sinful. Because God is so utterly different from us, we often need to talk about him in terms of what he's not. For example, we say that God is infinite—*not* finite. As creatures, we only can grasp finite things. When we say that God is infinite, it means he's not like anything else we deal with in life.

God reveals himself to us in his word, and that's where the creed gets the language of procession. So the creed, again, roots its teaching about God in the Bible. For such magnificent, transcendent truths, we want to stay very close to the language of the Scriptures.

The Spirit in Time

But the Bible also distinguishes the Holy Spirit from the Father and the Son in terms of what each Person does in human history. The Trinity always works together, but each Person plays a different role. And it's the Spirit, in many ways, that we know most directly in this age. The Spirit came down from heaven and empowered the church at Pentecost (Acts 2). The Spirit gives us new life, so we can respond to God in faith (John 3:5). The Spirit sanctifies us (Rom. 15:15–16).

The Spirit even lives inside us.

When warning the church about sexual immorality, the apostle Paul said, "Do you not know that your body is a temple of the Holy Spirit within you, whom you have from God? You are not your own, for you were bought with a price. So glorify God in your body" (1 Cor. 6:19–20). Why should we glorify God with our bodies? Because our bodies are temples of the Holy Spirit.

Who lived in the temple in ancient times? God. In the Old Testament, the temple in Jerusalem was God's place of residence. If our bodies are temples of the Holy Spirit, it means that God himself dwells in us. God the Holy Spirit lives inside his people. That's why we should be sexually pure—a temple is a holy place we must not defile.

---

2 Basil, "De Spiritu Sancto," https://www.newadvent.org/fathers/3203.htm.

The Spirit Who Speaks

The apostle Peter said, "For no prophecy was ever produced by the will of man, but men spoke from God as they were carried along by the Holy Spirit" (2 Pet. 1:21).

The prophets who foretold Jesus's coming spoke by the Holy Spirit. The Spirit inspired their words. They revealed things to God's people that the prophets could never have known if they relied on their own minds. The creed says that the Holy Spirit "spoke by the prophets." When the prophets spoke, the Holy Spirit spoke.

But, in fact, all of the Bible—not just the books we call "the prophets"—was inspired by the Holy Spirit. The Bible refers to Moses, who wrote the first five books of the Bible, as a prophet (Deut. 34:10). King David, who wrote many of the psalms, was also a prophet (Acts 2:29–30). "All Scripture," Paul said, "is God-breathed" (2 Tim. 3:16).

That's another distinct and crucial role of the Holy Spirit: he speaks God's word to us. Without the Spirit's inspiration of Scripture, we wouldn't know anything about the Trinity or what God has done to save us. The Nicene Creed depends on the Spirit-inspired word.

And at the center of the Spirit's revelation is Jesus Christ: "Long ago, at many times and in many ways, God spoke to our fathers by the prophets, but in these last days he has spoken to us by his Son" (Heb. 1:1–2). Jesus Christ is God's final word to us. And that word is brought to us through the inspired Scriptures. When we read the word or hear it preached, the Holy Spirit illuminates our minds, making us able to understand and believe what the Scriptures say about Christ.

When you hear God's word preached this Sunday, you'll encounter the Holy Spirit. He inspired the word. He enables you to understand it. And, if you're a Christian, he lives in you. God the Holy Spirit, equal in power and glory with the Father and the Son, unites you to God's final word, Jesus Christ. The Spirit works through the word, God's means of grace, to change you and complete God's work in your life.

Questions for Reflection

1. How does the Nicene Creed describe the relations of the Holy Spirit to God the Father and God the Son?

2. How does reflecting on the reality that the Holy Spirit lives in you affect how you view yourself and your life?

"I DO NOT ASK FOR THESE ONLY, BUT

ALSO FOR THOSE WHO WILL BELIEVE IN

ME THROUGH THEIR WORD, THAT THEY

MAY ALL BE ONE, JUST AS YOU, FATHER,

ARE IN ME, AND I IN YOU, THAT THEY

ALSO MAY BE IN US, SO THAT THE

WORLD MAY BELIEVE THAT YOU HAVE

SENT ME."

John 17:20–21

The *One* Holy Church

Read Acts 2:1–13; John 17:20

What Is Christ's Church Like?

The Holy Spirit is the Lord and Giver of Life. He is the third person of the Trinity, equal with the Father and the Son. And through the Holy Spirit, Jesus Christ created and sustains his church.

Before he died, Jesus told his disciples that he would send them the Holy Spirit (John 15:26–27). Then, on Pentecost, the Spirit came down:

> When the day of Pentecost arrived, they were all together in one place. And suddenly there came from heaven a sound like a mighty rushing wind, and it filled the entire house where they were sitting. And divided tongues as of fire appeared to them. And they were all filled with the Holy Spirit and began to speak in other tongues as the Spirit gave them utterance. (Acts 2:1–4)

The church was founded by Jesus Christ (Matt. 16:18). It was formed and empowered by the Holy Spirit (Acts 2). It continues to grow today, as the gospel spreads throughout the world.

But what is the church? What is it like? The Nicene Creed gives us a short statement that has been a lodestar for centuries: "I believe in the one holy catholic and apostolic church."

Two of these words may seem clear: *one* and *holy*. The other two, *catholic* and *apostolic*, may seem less clear. But each of these words leaves us with questions: How is the church one? How is it holy? How is it catholic and apostolic? Why did the Nicene Creed choose these words to describe our belief in Christ's church?

Do We Really Need the Church?

The word *church* comes from the Greek word *ecclesia*. It refers to an assembly or gathering. This points to the fact that God's people, his church, are called to gather together to worship God week after week (Acts 2:42–47; Heb. 10:25). If you belong to Jesus, you need to belong to a good local church, which is Christ's kingdom on Earth.

But today a lot of people dismiss the church. Fewer and fewer people even go to church. A recent study found that, for the first time ever, less than 50 percent of Americans attend church regularly. Even many professing Christians have a low view of the church.

There are many reasons for this. For example, in our consumeristic society, people have all kinds of things they can do on Sunday instead of going to church. For some people, Sunday is a day to kick back. For others, it's the day to load up at Costco, or perhaps it's just another day at the office. Few people can imagine giving up a chunk of their Sunday for church.

Other people just don't like anything that smacks of traditional authority. "Sure," they might say, "I believe in God. But I can worship him anywhere and any way I want. I don't need some priest or pastor telling me what to do."

Other people, understandably, have lost trust in the church because of the scandals that seem to keep coming to light. Again and again, we hear about pastors abusing their people or turning a blind eye when someone else abuses them. Sin doesn't disappear in the church and, sadly, the church's reputation has been damaged by her own failures.

Whatever the church's faults, her founder and head is Jesus. He hasn't abandoned her. He promised that he never will (Matt. 28:20).

And it's only *through* the church that any of us will reach our glorious destiny. The apostle Paul wrote, referring to Christ, "And he gave the apostles, the prophets, the evangelists, the shepherds and teachers, to equip the saints for the work of ministry, for building up the body of Christ, until we attain the unity of the faith and of the knowledge of the Son of God" (Eph. 4:11–13). Christ isn't building you up by yourself. He nurtures you and builds you up as one member in Christ's body. And his goal for us is "unity of the faith and the knowledge of the Son of God."

At the signing of the Declaration of Independence, Benjamin Franklin said to the other American founders, "We must, indeed, all hang together, or most assuredly we shall all hang separately."[1] He meant that the colonists needed to stay united. If they didn't, their revolution would fail, and each one of them would be hung as traitors to the British crown.

Likewise, Jesus Christ is building up his church as one body. He isn't building you or me as a free-floating foot or hand. We must—and will through the Spirit's power—hang together. We're only saved as part of Christ's body.

Is the Church the People or the Building?

Paul says that Christ gives his people gifts that nurture the body's growth: "the apostles, the prophets, the evangelists, the shepherds and teachers" (Eph. 4:11). God gives the church leaders who teach, guide, and govern her. They're weak and sinful. They're far from perfect. But those God calls to lead his church are gifts nonetheless. The Holy Spirit uses them to build up the body until it reaches its eternal unity in Christ.

As a pastor, I'm called to help people love Christ's church. If we love the church of Jesus Christ, we love and honor Christ. That's because the church is his body. We ought to have a high view of the church. We ought to love the church.

But, often, well-meaning Christians rightly point out that the church is the people of God and not the building we worship in. And if it's not the building, then we don't *go* to church, right? Wherever we *are* is the church. The church is wherever Christians are together. Didn't Jesus say, "Where two or three are gathered in my name, there I am among them" (Matt. 18:20)?

Yes, the church is the people of God. But God gathers his people through the visible church.

That visible church typically meets in a building to worship God together and is governed by pastors and elders. It is where the gospel is preached, new Christians are baptized, and the unrepentant are disciplined.

The visible church is where God has promised to work. It's his kingdom on earth.

It's wonderful to get together with other Christians for coffee or a Bible study. Christian fellowship is a beautiful and necessary thing. But it's not the same as gathering on Sunday as a member of a local church to hear the preached word, receive the Lord's Supper, and respond to God's grace with confession, prayer, and song.

---

1 Walter Isaacson, "Benjamin Franklin Joins the Revolution," https://www.smithsonianmag.com/history/benjamin-franklin-joins-the-revolution-87199988/.

A local, visible church is an embassy of the kingdom of God. Jesus Christ calls this church his bride, despite her many warts. God calls us to join it. And he promises to bless you when you do.

Questions for Reflection

1. Do you believe it's necessary to be part of a local, visible church? Why or why not?

2. How do you feel about the church? What experiences and beliefs have most shaped your attitude toward the church?

Read Ephesians 4:1; Psalm 133

The Church Is One

Just before Jesus went to the cross, he prayed for the church: "I do not ask for these only, but also for those who will believe in their word, that they may all be one, just as you Father are in me and I in you, that they also may be in us so that the world may believe that you have sent me" (John 17:20–21).

Jesus prayed for the oneness of the church. He wanted his church to be united. In fact, he said the church's unity would be a witness to the world. The church should be one "so that the world might know that you have sent me." Our unity testifies to the fact that God sent his Son into the world to suffer for our sins and rise again from the dead.

But when you look at the church today, you may not see unity. How can we confess that the church is one when we see Baptists and Presbyterians and Roman Catholics and Pentecostals and others divided?

Is there really one church of Christ?

Yes, there's one church. There's one church because there is one head of the church, one head of the body, our Lord Jesus Christ. And one Holy Spirit unites all believers to the head—and to each other.

How Is the Church One?

The Bible teaches that Jesus is the head of the church. The apostle Paul wrote, "And he is the head of the body, the church. He is the beginning, the firstborn from the dead, that in everything he might be preeminent" (Col. 1:18). That's the foundation of the church's unity.

I love the way the Protestant Reformer John put it: "There could not be two or three churches unless Christ be torn in pieces, which cannot happen. But all the elect are so united to Christ that they are dependent on one head. They also grow into one body being joined together as the limbs of a body."[2]

Unity, then, is not something that we have to create here on earth. Unity is a gift we receive. It's something we have in Christ. The church is one because she's united to one head, Jesus Christ. We're called to live in a way that's consistent with that reality. When we do, we make the gospel visible to the world.

That's what Paul said to the church in Ephesus. He told them to live "worthy of the calling" they had in Christ:

> I, therefore, a prisoner for the Lord, urge you to walk in a manner worthy of the calling to which you have been called, with all humility and gentleness, with patience, bearing with one another in love, eager to maintain the unity of the Spirit in the bond of peace. There is one body and one Spirit—just as you were called to the one hope that belongs to your call—one Lord, one faith, one baptism, one God and Father of all, who is over all and through all and in all. (Eph. 4:1–6)

Oneness comes to us from God. There's "one body and one Spirit." Unity comes from above. And we're called to live in a way that fits with the spiritual unity we have.

Brothers and sisters, we're called to live as one. We're called to be reconciled with one another. We're called to pursue peace with each other in the church. We do this because God has given us his peace through his Son, Jesus Christ (Rom. 5:1).

Unity: Local or Global?

So, is this oneness mainly local? Is it mainly about getting along with people in your church? Or does the call to Christian unity mean that the whole church around the world should be one?

If Christ is the one head of the one church, then we're called to pursue oneness both in our local churches and in the universal church—the church around the world. I'm a pastor of a local church. I hope you're a part of a local church. But we're also part of the universal church with all who call on the name of Jesus Christ.

But this doesn't mean that the church can or should be united in a single global institution. The church is both local and universal. It's also both visible and invisible. The visible church is the church we see. It's the churches' pastors and buildings and congregations and budgets. These visible churches are pure to different degrees. They're united to different degrees. The visible church includes some members who have never really trusted in Christ.

God calls us into his visible church. That's where we receive the grace of preaching, the sacraments,

---

2 John Calvin, *The Institutes of the Christian Religion*, IV 1.2.

and Christian nurture. Cyprian of Carthage, who lived in the century before the Council of Nicaea, taught that "outside of the church there is no salvation."[3] That doesn't mean the church saves us. It means that Christ saves us through the church. To reject the church is to reject Christ because the church is his body.

The invisible church is all those, in every age, who have truly trusted in Christ. Only God sees this invisible church. That's because, unlike us, God sees the heart of every individual (1 Sam. 16:7). He knows those who are his (2 Tim. 2:19). This invisible church is unified in Christ.

One Faith, One Baptism

So with the Nicene Creed, we confess that the church is one. We affirm the unity that we have in Jesus Christ, the head of the church. This unity exists through faith and baptism: "For just as the body is one and has many members, and all the members of the body, though many, are one body, so it is with Christ. For in one Spirit we were all baptized into one body—Jews or Greeks, slaves or free—and all were made to drink of one Spirit" (1 Cor. 12:12–13).

Christ is the head of the church. So there can only be one church. If we're united to Jesus, we're a part of his body. The visible church of Christ may look like it's torn in shreds. But we confess one true faith, in one Lord, through one Spirit. And we do this when we confess the Nicene Creed, which the church has confessed since ancient times. The rule of faith unites us across the globe and through time, despite the many divisions that remain.

Questions for Reflection

1. How do we know that the church is one, regardless of how things look?

2. Where have you seen evidence of unity in your local church?

---

3 Cyprian, "Epistle 72," https://www.newadvent.org/fathers/050672.htm

Read John 15:1–11

The Church Is Holy

The church of Christ is one. It's united in Christ. The Nicene Creed also says that the church is holy.

Like the belief that the church is one, the idea that the church is holy might seem like a denial of the visible facts. Think about all the scandals, all of the pastors involved in terrible things, all the sin that's so obvious in the church. Think about your own heart. How can we say that the church is holy? It's grievous to think about many things that have happened among God's people.

Still, we confess that the church is holy. What does the creed mean by this? What makes the church holy?

Who Makes Us Holy?

When you think of holiness, you may picture figures in white robes with glowing heads. We've inherited cultural images of people or supernatural beings with an otherworldly form of moral purity.

This idea isn't entirely wrong. Holiness is otherworldly. It reflects the holy character of the transcendent God. The Bible itself gives us the image of holy people wearing white robes (Rev. 6:11).

But the images we may know from Renaissance paintings or stained-glass windows also can be misleading. The church isn't holy, first and foremost, because of her own moral purity. The church is holy because she is united to Christ.

The church is the communion of saints. That word *saints*, in some Christian traditions, refers to a special class of sanctified people—the holy, glowing figures that may pop into our minds. That's what Roman Catholic and Eastern Orthodox churches usually mean when they talk about saints.

But in the Bible, the saints are those who are united to Jesus. For example, the apostle Paul wrote a letter to a church in the Greek city of Corinth. The Corinthian church had a lot of problems. Paul needed to call out their sexual sin, pride, and divisions. He began the letter, though, by calling them saints: "To the church of God that is in Corinth, to those sanctified in Christ Jesus, called to be saints" (1 Cor. 1:2). He called them saints and "those sanctified." That means they're already holy, even though they've got big problems.

Paul again called them sanctified later in the same letter: "You were washed, you were sanctified, you were justified in the name of the Lord Jesus Christ and by the Spirit of our God" (1 Cor. 6:11). Just as the church received her oneness from above, so the church is holy because Jesus Christ shares his holiness with us. That's why even the Corinthians—even you and I—are saints. In spite of our big problems with sin, we're holy because we're united to Christ by faith.

The church is holy even though—in this age—she's still sinful.

The book of Hebrews addresses another troubled church. Some of the Hebrews were tempted to abandon Christ and return to the Jewish law. They seemed to be on the verge of throwing the gospel out the window. But the writer of the letter called them "holy brothers" (Heb. 3:1).

By virtue of her faith in Jesus Christ, the church is holy. All Christians are saints. We're all sanctified in Jesus Christ by the grace of the Holy Spirit.

Holiness refers to the status we have when God sets us apart as his own. It's given to us, and then we grow into holiness as we live by faith.

Being Holy and Becoming Holy

We're called the holy ones. We're called saints.

But we're also called to *become* holy. God says, "You shall be holy, for I am holy." (1 Pet. 1:16). The book of Hebrews says, "Strive for peace with everyone and for the holiness without which no one will see the Lord" (Heb. 12:14). We're holy now and forever because of our union with Christ, but we're called to become holy, like him.

This growing holiness, like our holy status, comes from our union with Christ. Jesus told his disciples, "I am the vine; you are the branches. Whoever abides in me and I in him, he it is that bears much fruit, for apart from me you can do nothing" (John 15:5). In our daily lives, we become more holy, more sanctified over time. And this happens because we're branches attached to Jesus, the vine.

And it's the Holy Spirit, working through the word of God, who both unites us to Christ and keeps us united to Christ. Through the work of the Spirit, we "abide" in Christ. Sanctification—our growth in holiness—is the work of the Holy Spirit. But if we try to become holy apart from faith in Christ and his work of salvation, we'll utterly fail: "Apart from me you can do nothing."

The church's holiness, then, like its unity, is a gift from God. We're not called holy mainly because of our otherworldly moral purity. We're not saints because we're righteous or perfect in our hearts and actions right now. We're holy now because we're united to the holy one, who is also making us holy (Eph. 5:25–31).

When we say the church is holy, we're saying she is different because of what God has done."

We're not holy because of what we've done. God makes us holy. We're saints because of what God has done for us in his Son Jesus Christ. The gospel makes the church holy.

The Hope of Holiness

Since the holiness of the Christian comes from Christ, we confess the church's holiness by faith. But by confessing the church's holiness through the words of the Nicene Creed, we also confess our hope. That's because we look forward to the perfect and spotless holiness we're going to have in the presence of God in the new creation.

In this life, the Holy Spirit transforms us. He sanctifies us. In the life to come, that work will be finished. We'll be fully transformed into the likeness of Christ (1 John 3:2). We'll be glorified. And as his holy people, we'll worship the holy God forever.

Questions for Reflection

1. How is the church holy?

2. When have you *seen* holiness in the church?

"AFTER THIS I LOOKED, AND BEHOLD, A
GREAT MULTITUDE THAT NO ONE COULD
NUMBER, FROM EVERY NATION, FROM ALL
TRIBES AND PEOPLES AND LANGUAGES,
STANDING BEFORE THE THRONE AND
BEFORE THE LAMB, CLOTHED IN WHITE
ROBES, WITH PALM BRANCHES IN THEIR
HANDS."

Revelation 7:9

What Do *Catholic* and *Apostolic* Mean?

Read Isaiah 2:1–5

Christ's Church Is Catholic

Once every few months, someone will walk up to me after our church service with a suspicious look on his face. The person will point to the line in the Nicene Creed, which we print in our church bulletin, that confesses, "I believe in one holy catholic and apostolic church."

"Right here," the person will say, "it says that you believe in the catholic church." They'll look at me wondering, "What kind of a church is this? Is this a Roman Catholic Church?"

We've seen that the Nicene Creed lists four attributes, or characteristics, of the church. In addition to being one and holy, the church is also catholic and apostolic. But what do those words *catholic* and *apostolic* mean? They're not everyday words. And they may at first seem to refer to things other than what the Bible teaches about the church.

Catholic means *universal*. The catholic church is the universal church of Christ, the church that's spread throughout the earth and across the centuries. That's what's the Nicene Creed means when it says, "I believe in one holy catholic and apostolic church."

The Church Includes All Kinds of People

The church is catholic in a few different, but overlapping, ways.

First, *catholic* refers to the people in the church. The church isn't made up of just one ethnicity or political alignment.

In the Old Testament, Israel was a single people: one nation and culture set apart by God. God rescued Israel out of Egypt and made a covenant with them at Mount Sinai. This covenant, which established the terms of God's relationship with his people, was called the Mosaic Covenant or, after Jesus came, the Old Covenant. Through this covenant, God made Israel his holy nation.

But the gospel of Jesus Christ goes out to the whole world (Matt. 28:18–20; Acts 1:8). Jesus is the universal King. His kingdom, the church, includes all kinds of people.

One of the great promises in the prophets begins this way:

> It shall come to pass in the latter days
> > that the mountain of the house of the Lord
> shall be established as the highest of the mountains,
> > and shall be lifted up above the hills;
> and all the nations shall flow to it,
> > and many people shall come and say: "Come, let us go to the mountain of the
> > > Lord,
> > to the house of the God of Jacob,
> that he may teach us his ways
> > and that we may walk in his paths. (Isa. 2:2–3a)

Isaiah said that a time will come when the whole world will ascend Mount Zion, the heavenly Jerusalem (Heb. 12:22–24). People from every tribe, tongue, and nation will gather to worship the Triune God.

That's what we experience under the New Covenant—the relationship that God established with everyone who trusts in Christ. That's what we look forward to when we gather together for church on Sunday.

- The book of Revelation offers another vision of this future global worship: "After this, I looked and behold, a great multitude that no one could number, from every nation, from all tribes and peoples and languages standing before the throne and before the Lamb, clothed in white robes, with palm branches in their hands" (Rev. 7:9).

The Bible gives us these beautiful pictures of the catholic church. In the New Covenant, the gentiles—non-Jews—are welcomed into the faith of God's people. They're adopted into God's family. This caused major controversies in the early church because most of the first Christians were Jews. But the inclusion of the gentiles showed that Jesus had united all peoples, bringing them together to worship the true and the living God.

The apostle Paul wrote,

> Therefore remember that at one time you Gentiles in the flesh, called the uncircumcision by what is called the circumcision, which is made in the flesh by hands—remember that you were at that time separated from Christ, alienated from the commonwealth of Israel and strangers to the covenants of promise, having no hope and without God in the world. But now in Christ Jesus you who once were far off have been brought near by the blood of Christ. For he himself is our peace, who has made us both one and has broken down in his flesh the dividing wall of hostility. (Eph. 2:11–14)

In the New Covenant, no one is excluded based on their race, ethnicity, gender, culture, or anything else. The gospel goes out to everyone; all who put their faith in Christ become part of God's people. We're "brought near by the blood of Christ."

The Light of the Whole World

But this catholicity didn't come out of nowhere in the new covenant. When God chose Abraham and made a covenant with him, he said, "Your name shall be Abraham, for I have made you the father of a multitude of nations. I will make you exceedingly fruitful, and I will make you into nations, and kings shall come from you" (Gen. 17:5–6).

Before making Abraham "the father of a multitude of nations," he made him the father of *one* nation, Israel. But God called Israel to be "a light to the nations" (Isa. 49:6). God's Old Covenant people were supposed to bless the world.

That light often flickered out, and God judged Israel. But God kept his promise. Jesus the Messiah was a Jew. He came as "the true light, which gives light to everyone" (John 1:9). All who believe in him are the true Israel, the true sons of Abraham (Gal. 3:7–9), regardless of the earthly nation they call home.

Our churches should reflect this catholicity. The church of Christ isn't an affinity group. We don't go to church to hang out with people just like us. We're not called to love only those who look like us and think like us and have piercings in the same places we do. Churches are hospitals for every kind of person. We gather together around the throne of God and of the Lamb to worship with our brothers and sisters from all over the world, from all different cultures and backgrounds.

That's the catholic church.

Questions for Reflection

1. How is the New Covenant church different from the Old Covenant nation of Israel?

2. When you think about your local church, how catholic does it look?

Read John 4:7–30

Christ's Church Is Everywhere

The church is catholic, or universal, because it welcomes every kind of person. It isn't just for Jews or any other single ethnicity. But since it includes all kinds of people, the church is also catholic in another sense: location. The catholic church is everywhere on earth.

The true church isn't just in Jerusalem. It's not just in Rome. It's not just among the persecuted believers in China or Iran. It's not just in Alabama.

Under the Old Covenant, the worship of God focused on one place—the temple in Jerusalem. People flocked to Jerusalem to observe the feasts and participate in the sacrifices. But we don't have that kind of temple today. The temple in Jerusalem was a picture, a type or shadow, of a greater reality. It pointed to Christ.

The temple of God today is the people of God. And this temple is throughout the world.

The Hour Has Now Come

Once, Jesus spoke to a woman who came to get water from a well. Jesus asked her for a drink, and they started talking. As Jesus began showing he knew the hidden details of her life, she said, "Sir, I perceive that you are a prophet. Our fathers worshiped on this mountain, but you say that in Jerusalem is the place where people ought to worship" (John 4:19–20). This woman wasn't Jewish. She was a Samaritan, and therefore unwelcome in Jewish society. And she brought up the conflict between Jews and Samaritans regarding the right place to worship.

Jesus said to her:

The hour is coming when neither on this mountain nor in Jerusalem will you worship the

Father. You worship what you do not know; we worship what we know, for salvation is from the Jews. But the hour is coming and is now here, when the true worshipers will worship the Father in spirit and in truth, for the Father is seeking such people to worship him. (John 4:21–23)

In the New Covenant, Jesus told her, people will worship the true God everywhere. Under the Old Covenant, God made the temple in Jerusalem the center of worship. But that was only for a time. Jesus said that "the hour is coming and is now here" when that will change. In fact, his presence signified this change of the ages.

This change brings the catholicity of people and place together. The new temple is everywhere because, through Christ, God's "true worshipers" are now everywhere. The worshipers are the temple. You and I are "living stones" in the new temple God is building (1 Pet. 2:5).

The Church's Universal Teaching

This universal church—this church that's everywhere—holds to catholic doctrine. In other words, the catholic church is identified by its teaching.

In the fifth century, a man named Vincent of Lerins wrote that all possible care must be taken to believe that which has been believed everywhere. This idea of catholic doctrine helps us identify heresy even today. We need to embrace the core, catholic doctrines in the Nicene Creed: the Trinity, the two natures of Christ, Jesus's works of salvation, and the Spirit of God's work in the church.

This is the doctrine we need to embrace. If your church believes something about the Bible that no one has believed for 2000 years, it probably isn't catholic. Yes, differences exist among Christian traditions, but the Nicene Creed gives us a baseline. Christians from the times of the apostles have embraced these catholic doctrines as a baton and handed them down again and again and again.

This is the deepest and purest stream of Christian orthodoxy. We're called to drink from these safe waters. They're safe waters in a world that is spiritually thirsty. We come to this wellspring of sound doctrine to be restored.

If your church doesn't teach this catholic doctrine, that's a real problem.

Years ago, during a church planting conference in Salt Lake City, I went with a couple of other guys to check out the Mormon history museum. This museum had big murals of events in the life of Jesus, like when he fed the 5,000 and walked on the water. After this series of New Testament scenes, we came to a bare black wall. No pictures, just black. Then after the black wall, more murals appeared. These next murals showed Joseph Smith, the founder of the Mormons, and events related to the Book of Mormon.

We asked the tour guide, "What's the deal with this? You have the pictures of Jesus from the New Testament and then this big black wall and then these murals of Joseph Smith." He said, "The big black wall is a picture of the dark years of the church, where the gospel was snuffed out. The gospel was lost after the book of Acts, and then it was restored by Joseph Smith."

So, according to this museum, for over 1,500 years no one followed the Bible's teaching. Basically, there were no Christians between the apostle Paul and Joseph Smith. But that doesn't fit with the belief in one, holy, catholic, and apostolic church.

And it doesn't fit with the New Testament. Jesus said: "I will build my church, and the gates of hell shall not prevail again against it" (Matt. 16:18). He also said, "I am with you always, to the end of the age" (Matt. 28:20). Jesus didn't say anything about a 1,500-year black wall. He said nothing about a dark age when the gospel would be lost or the need for a new revelation in some far off future.

How To Stay Safely in the Sheepfold

Yes, the gospel has often been threatened. At times, the darkness has seemed to be winning. But Jesus Christ promised to build his church, to defend her, and to be with her always. We know that the church was and always will be, because the one who's building the church isn't you or me. It's Jesus Christ. And the bricks of God's temple, the church, come from every tribe, tongue, and nation on earth.

The church is universal. Her doctrine is universal. Embracing the doctrine that has been believed by all true churches of Christ keeps us from wandering into the darkness of heresy.

Questions for Reflection

1. What does it mean to say that a doctrine is catholic?

2. Have you ever thought you discovered a new biblical teaching or been in a church that focused on doctrines it claimed were new or unique? If so, how did you evaluate these ideas?

Read Acts 2:42; Galatians 1:6–9

The Apostolic Church

Christ's church is one, holy, catholic, and apostolic. What does apostolic mean? It must have something to do with the apostles, right? But how, exactly, do the apostles give the church its nature?

Different church traditions define *apostolicity* in different ways. For example, the Roman Catholic and Eastern Orthodox churches believe that apostolicity refers to something called apostolic succession. There's been an unbroken line of bishops since the apostles, they say, and this lineage guarantees the purity of the church's teachings.

But no unbroken line of bishops, priests, or pastors ensures that the church has kept pure, apostolic teaching. Instead, the word of God, written by the apostles and prophets through the inspiration of the Holy Spirit, ensures that the church can always hold fast to the apostles' teaching.

Where Do We Find the Apostles' Teaching?

The catechism of the Roman Catholic Church says that the Catholic Church is apostolic in three ways.[1] The church is apostolic, first, because she was "built on the foundation of the apostles and prophets" (Eph. 2:20).

Second, the church is apostolic because, with the help of the Holy Spirit dwelling in her, the church "keeps and hands on the teaching, the 'good deposit,' the salutary words she has heard from the apostles."[2]

These first two ways are fine. They're biblical.

It's the third idea that's a problem. The Catholic catechism says that the church "continues to be taught, sanctified, and guided by the apostles until Christ's return, through their successors in pastoral office: in the college of bishops, 'assisted by priests, in union with the successor of Peter, the church's supreme pastor.'"[3] This means that the church's apostolicity depends on the living presence of the apostles in the current bishops of the church and the pope.

That's the Roman Catholic doctrine of apostolicity. But that's not what the Bible teaches.

About 500 years ago, the Protestant Reformers argued against the Roman Catholic teaching on apostolicity. They said that the church isn't apostolic because of a succession of people in the ministry linked to the apostles through the laying on of hands. Instead, there's an apostolic succession of preaching. You're not apostolic because you're somehow spiritually related to the apostles; you're apostolic because you preach what the apostles preached.

And we know what the apostles preached by reading the word of God.

This is where the words of the apostle Paul ring true. He said that the church is built on the foundation of the apostles and prophets (Eph. 2:20), and we find that foundation in the words they have left to us: the Scripture.

Also think of what our Lord Jesus said to Peter. After Peter confessed that Jesus is the Christ, Jesus said, "Blessed are you, Simon Bar-Jonah! For flesh and blood has not revealed this to you, but my Father who is in heaven" (Matt. 16:17). That confession of the truth is the foundation for the church. And that truth, which the apostles preached and gave to us, is found in the holy word of God.

The Apostolic Message

Apostolicity, then, is a succession of the apostles' preaching and teaching. We need the grace of God in the pure preaching of the gospel to bring life to the world and life to the church. The gospel makes a ministry apostolic. We're apostolic if we preach the doctrine of the apostles.

Paul gave the Galatian church this warning: "Even if we, or an angel from heaven, should preach to

---

1 *Catechism of the Catholic Church*, p. 247, par. 857.
2 *Catechism of the Catholic Church*, p. 246, par. 857.
3 *Catechism of the Catholic Church*, p. 246, par. 857.

you a gospel contrary to the one we preached to you, let him be accursed" (Gal. 1:8). In effect, Paul was saying, "Look, even if we *apostles* preach something different than what we already taught you, we're under a curse. God gave us one message to preach, and if we mess with it, we'll answer to God. In fact, don't even believe an angel if he preaches something other than the gospel of Christ."

It's the gospel message, not the messenger, that matters. The message makes the church apostolic.

In Acts 2, the first Christians "devoted themselves to the apostles' teaching and the fellowship, to the breaking of the bread and the prayers" (Acts 2:42). The "breaking of the bread" probably refers to the Lord's Supper. This beautiful picture of the earliest apostolic church shows us what our churches need to be committed to today. These things—the apostles' teaching, the sacraments, and prayer—are what the one, holy, catholic, and apostolic church does.

Is your church apostolic? Does your church cling to the teaching of the apostles revealed in Scripture?

We confess in the Nicene Creed that the church is one, holy, catholic, and apostolic. It was in Acts 2 and it still is today. Christ guides and guards his church and its apostolic teaching through the Holy Spirit, who inspired the written words of the prophets and apostles. The same Spirit illuminates the minds of Christians today, and in every age, so that we can grasp and believe the apostolic gospel, the "word of life" (Phil. 2:16).

Questions for Reflection

1.   What does *apostolic* mean?

2.   How do we know if a church is devoted to the apostles' teachings?

"HOW THEN WILL THEY CALL ON HIM IN

WHOM THEY HAVE NOT BELIEVED? AND

HOW ARE THEY TO BELIEVE IN HIM OF

WHOM THEY HAVE NEVER HEARD? AND HOW

ARE THEY TO HEAR WITHOUT SOMEONE

PREACHING?"

_____

Romans 10:14

How Do I *Find* a *Good* Church?

Read 2 Corinthians 2:5–11; 1 Peter 1:23; Hebrews 4:12–13

What Should You Look For In a Church?

Christ's church is one, holy, catholic, and apostolic. We find these characteristics throughout the pages of the Bible. Because the Nicene Creed is a faithful, historical summary of Christian doctrine, we should look for a church that believes, teaches, and embodies the instruction of the creed.

But are these characteristics always visible? Are they obvious from the outside? If we're looking for a good church, one that teaches "the faith that was once for all delivered to the saints" (Jude 3), how do we know when we see one?

A true church of Christ can be identified by certain marks. These marks are things you can check for yourself. You can go to a church and ask yourself, "Do I see these marks or not?" These marks are vital and practical because we need to be plugged into solid, Bible-believing churches. These show us what to look for.

What Are the Marks of the Church?

People often wonder, "What should I look for in a church?" Should you focus on the style of music? Whether the pastor is a good communicator or is funny? Should you focus on the order of the worship service? Should you be concerned about the ministries of church for the youth, elderly, those with disabilities, and so on? Does it matter whether the church has ministries that meet the specific needs of your family?

Those are all good questions. But the most important question is, "What does the church teach? How does the church administer the sacraments? Does the church practice appropriate discipline?"

Thinking about the marks of the church can be sobering. It's sobering to me as a pastor. Jesus told Peter, "I tell you, you are Peter, and on this rock, I will build my church and the gates of hell shall not prevail against it. I will give you the keys of the kingdom of heaven, and whatever you bind on earth shall be bound in heaven, and whatever you loose on earth shall be loosed in heaven" (Matt. 16:18–19).

Think about that responsibility. Jesus gave his church the keys to the kingdom of heaven.

Imagine somebody giving you the keys to his new Lamborghini. If you're not used to driving $300,000 cars, you may feel a little worried. Taking care of that beautiful car is a great responsibility. That's a little bit like the responsibility given to Peter and the apostles. Jesus told them, "Here, I'm giving you the keys."

But what are the keys to the kingdom? It's not that the church itself decides who God will save. Instead, it means Christ gave his church the responsibility to do three main things: preach the word, administer the sacraments, and practice church discipline. Through these tasks, the gospel goes out to the world, new believers enter the church, and the people of God grow in their faith.

Jesus, of course, didn't leave the church alone with this responsibility. He said, "I am with you to the end of the age" (Matt. 28:20). Jesus rules the church as her king. He remains present with the church through the Holy Spirit. He governs and guides the church through his word, the Bible.

But it's still a sobering responsibility. That's why James said, "Not many of you should become teachers, my brothers, for you know that we who teach will be judged with greater strictness" (James 3:1).

And that's one reason we've been thinking about the rule of faith, passing on the apostolic baton. Paul wrote to Timothy about guarding the good deposit of faith and entrusting it to others. Jude called us to contend for the faith "once for all delivered to the saints"—to protect the holy gospel.

What Is Preaching?

The marks of the church, then, help identify the church's responsibility. And it helps us see whether a church is faithful to that responsibility. Jesus Christ entrusted his church with the word, the sacraments, and discipline. You should be looking for a church that practices all three of these things.

Preaching is often called the first mark of the church. Of course, a church isn't a true church just because someone stands behind a pulpit and talks. Jesus called his church to preach *the gospel*. He gave his church the responsibility of preaching the Bible truthfully and clearly.

John Calvin asked, "Why do we willfully act like madmen in searching out the church? When Christ has marked it out with an unmistakable sign, which wherever it is seen, cannot fail to show the church there, while where it is absent, nothing remains that can give the true Church meaning."[1]

What "unmistakable sign" is Calvin talking about? The pure preaching of the gospel. That's the foundational mark of the true church.

The Living Word

We saw that the church is "built on the foundation of the apostles and prophets" (Eph. 2:20). In other words, it's built on their message—their preaching. And what did the apostles preach? Christ and the gospel. The prophets spoke about Christ before he came. The apostles gave the full revelation of Christ.

When you visit a church, listen for the gospel, the good news that Christ died for our sins and rose again. That's the primary mark of the true church.

You can't have the church without this mark because God creates the church through his word. Just as God spoke the world into being, he speaks the church into being. Through the word of God, we're born again: "You have been born again, not of perishable seed but of imperishable, through the living and abiding word of God" (1 Pet. 1:23). The word creates faith in our hearts. It creates a people of faith who gather to worship God "in spirit and truth" (John 4:24).

The word of God isn't just information about Jesus. It's a life-giving power. Through the word, the Holy Spirit brings forth new life in us. The apostle Paul wrote, "Faith comes from hearing and hearing by the word of Christ" (Rom. 10:17). Isaiah wrote:

> For as the rain and snow come down from heaven
>   and do not return there but water the earth,
> making it bring forth and sprout,
>   giving seed to the sower and bread to the eater,
> so shall my word be that goes forth from my mouth;

---

1 Calvin, *Institutes*, IV 2.4.

> it shall not return to me empty,
> but shall accomplish that which I purpose, and shall succeed in the thing for which
> I sent it. (Isa. 55:10–11)

Throughout the Bible, we see this idea that God's word is "living and active" (Heb. 4:12). Through the word of God, the heavens and the earth were made and faith is created in our hearts through the proclamation of the gospel.

A church without the pure preaching of the word of God is not a church.

How Should We Listen to Sermons?

If a church doesn't preach the gospel, it's not a true church. If a church believes in some other way of salvation, it's not a true church. A church can have a nice building. The clergy might get all dressed up and look great. In the church's services every week, someone may get up in front of everyone and crack jokes or talk about the latest hot-button social issues. But if the gospel isn't preached, then that gathering is just a club. Those people may like each other's company and even do good things in the community, but they're not a true church.

Jesus Christ told his church to proclaim the word of God. He called his church to preach the gospel. Only the gospel gives real spiritual life and vitality. For the sake of our souls, we need to be in churches that clearly teach the word of God. The word alone gives birth to faith in our hearts and nourishes that faith day by day by day.

But we're also called to get ready to hear the preached word. I love the way the Westminster Larger Catechism puts it. This time-tested teaching tool of the church asks us, "What is required of those that hear the Word preached?" Then it gives the biblical answer: "It is required of those that hear the Word preached, that they attend upon it with diligence, preparation, and prayer; examine what they hear by the Scriptures; receive the truth with faith, love, meekness, and readiness of mind, as the Word of God; meditate, and confer of it; hide it in their hearts, and bring forth the fruit of it in their lives" (WLC 160).

The power to bring forth new life is in the word of God. But that doesn't mean we do nothing. We pray, we "examine" the biblical passages we hear preached, we embrace what the word says, we hang onto it in our hearts, and we live out the new life we receive. This too, is the work of the Holy Spirit who works in us (Phil. 2:12–13).

What Do You Hear?

The word creates the church. We're called to receive the word with humility. We're called to pray, "God open my eyes, open my heart, illuminate my mind to receive the truth of your word."

God's word brings life. That's a beautiful thing for us to meditate on.

So the first mark of the church is the pure preaching the word of God, the preaching of the gospel. Where the word of God is preached, the church of Jesus Christ exists. Where it isn't preached, you might have a group of people getting together, but you don't have a true church.

Questions for Reflection

1. What is true preaching? Why is this mark essential for the church?

2. How do you usually listen to sermons? How do you prepare for them? What do you usually do after you hear a sermon?

Read 1 Corinthians 11:23–26; Matthew 28:19

What Are the Sacraments?

Some people hear the word *sacrament* and think, "Okay, this sounds sort of Roman Catholic or something." But the Protestant churches of the Reformation practiced the sacraments and kept using that word: *sacrament*. So what is a sacrament, exactly?

The term *sacrament* comes from a Latin translation of the Greek word *mysterion*, which means *mystery*. The sacraments are the mysteries of the faith. The church must steward these mysteries. That's the responsibility that Jesus gave to the apostles and those who would later lead the church.

The "mysteries of the faith" refers to the ways in which God mysteriously works in the lives of people today. The Holy Spirit gives grace to his people through the ordinary means of baptism and the Lord's Supper. The Spirit makes Jesus Christ spiritually present in these practices. God has attached his name to these things, and he calls us to come to be built up by the grace he offers through them.

Are the Sacraments Biblical?

We practice the sacraments because Jesus commanded the church to practice them (Luke 22:19; Matt. 28:19). The Bible reveals two sacraments: baptism and the Lord's Supper. The Roman Catholic Church believes there are seven sacraments. The additional five sacraments that Catholics practice aren't in the Bible; the Catholic church adopted them hundreds of years later.

When the Nicene Creed states, "I believe in one Baptism for the remission of sins," it echoes the apostle Peter. On the day of Pentecost, when the Holy Spirit came down from heaven and empowered the church, Peter said, "Repent and be baptized every one of you in the name of Jesus Christ for the forgiveness of sins, and you will receive the gift of the Holy Spirit" (Acts 2:38).

A sacrament includes both a sign and a spiritual reality that the sign points to. The bread and wine are the signs of the Lord's Supper. They point to a spiritual reality: Jesus himself. When we eat the bread and drink the wine by faith, we feed on Jesus himself and all of his benefits.

The sign and the thing the sign points to are closely related, but they're not the same. The bread and wine don't physically change into the body and blood of Christ. But we do truly feed on Jesus spiritually. It's not just that we're thinking about Jesus and remembering what he did for us. When we eat and drink, we're *spiritually* nourished. We feed on Christ and all he is for us.

The sacraments, then, are mainly God's actions toward us rather than something we do. A sacrament is God's visible word, his visible gospel. It washes us, nourishes us, and feeds us in the Christian life. The sacraments are *secondarily* our profession of faith, but first and foremost, they're God's actions towards us, his people. Every time you see someone baptized, every time you eat and drink the Lord's Supper, God moves, speaks, and gives himself to his people.

Receiving the Seal of the King

People often ask me, "How can I know that I'm a Christian? I struggle with sin. I struggle to believe that I'm forgiven. How can I know? I look inside, and everything's still messed up. Yes, I believe in Jesus. I'm even a member of the church. But I still wonder if God's grace is really for me."

Maybe you've felt that. Maybe you've gone to church and heard the pastor preaching the gospel. He talked about the love of Jesus, and it seemed easy to believe that Jesus's love was for the others in the room. You thought those other people—even though you didn't know all their sins—were probably easier to love than you are. It can be hard to believe the love of Jesus is really for you.

So how can you be sure?

Through the sacraments. The sacraments aren't just signs. They're seals. Just as a king stamps an official document with his seal, God stamps his people through the sacraments. When you receive the sacraments, you hear God saying to you: "You're mine. You belong to me."

A seal certifies the reality of something. When God seals you through the sacraments, he pledges his goodwill, his love, and his gospel promise to you.

God gives us the sacraments—these visible signs, these tokens of his love—to nourish our faith and reassure us. As you take the sign of bread and wine, you hear Jesus say, "This is my body given for you. This is my blood shed for you." If by faith we receive these signs, we have the spiritual reality. It's as if God himself is saying to his people, "This grace is for you. I know you struggle. I know you're weighed down by your sins. But my grace is for *you*. My grace is as real as these visible signs you eat and drink."

The sacraments were instituted by Christ, and he commanded the church to observe them. For that reason, a true church will practice the sacraments in the way Jesus taught.

Questions for Reflection

1. What are the sacraments? How do we know which sacraments are biblical?

2. How does your church talk about and practice the sacraments?

Read Matthew 18:15–18; 2 Corinthians 2:5–11

What's Church Discipline?

The three marks of the church are the preaching of the gospel, the right use of the sacraments, and church discipline.

But you might be wondering about church discipline in particular. Even before reading these lessons, you likely knew what preaching is. You were probably familiar with the sacraments: baptism and the Lord's Supper. Discipline, though, may be pretty vague. It may even sound threatening. Maybe you think of the Spanish Inquisition or some other form of menacing church power.

Jesus taught the apostles about church discipline. Not long after he gave them the keys to the kingdom (Matt. 16:18–19), he said:

> If your brother sins against you go and tell him his fault between you and him alone. If he listens to you, you have gained your brother. But if he does not listen, take one or two others along with you, that every charge may be established by the evidence of two or three witnesses. If he refuses to listen to them, tell it to the church. And if he refuses to listen even to the church, let him be to you as a Gentile and a tax collector. Truly, I say to you, whatever you bind on earth shall be bound in heaven, and whatever you loose on earth, shall be loosed in heaven. (Matt. 18:15–18)

Basically, Jesus teaches them about how to deal with sin in the church. Christians should first try to resolve any problems among themselves. But if they can't, they should bring the issue to the leaders of the church. If someone has committed a major sin and refuses to repent of it even to the church, then the church needs to begin taking steps toward excommunicating that person—removing him from the church.

Jesus said that excommunication is part of the responsibility of having the keys. Just as the preaching of the gospel opens the door to one and all, calling everyone to believe the gospel and enter the church, church discipline closes the door to church members who refuse to live as Christians.

The church needs to guard its purity—especially the purity of the gospel message. When the church allows sin to fester, sin's destructive influence spreads.

And that's no secret at this point. We've been inundated in recent years with news about churches who refused to discipline leaders and members. Abuse of women and children, bullying, racism, and other sins have been waved away, excused, or hidden, which has often just allowed those guilty of these sins to abuse or bully more people. Sadly, it often takes a terrible public scandal before churches take any real steps to hold people accountable.

But church discipline *isn't* about reviving the Spanish Inquisition. In fact, it isn't anything like the punishment that the rest of the world metes out to wrongdoers (Rom. 13:1–8). If a church member has committed a crime, it needs to be reported to the proper authorities. That church member needs to accept whatever punishment the civil government deems fitting. The church, though, doesn't "bear the sword" (Matt. 26:52; Rom 13:3–4). Jesus *didn't* give the church authority to punish anyone, especially not through any kind of violence or blackmail.

And if a church excommunicates someone, that doesn't mean that person's soul is lost forever. Christians first enter the church through faith and repentance, and they *return* to the church through faith and repentance. If a Christian loses his membership in the church, it's because he has refused to confess his sin and embrace the grace of God in Christ. But the moment he truly repents, the church must embrace him once again (2 Cor. 2:5–11).

The church is a place for sinners. Her arms—like the arms of her Lord—are wide open for those who confess their sins and trust in the gospel of grace.

How Do We Nourish Christian Hope?

So these are the marks of the church: preaching, the sacraments, and discipline. If you see that a church practices these three things in a biblical way, it's a true church. Through these marks, the Holy Spirit creates and builds the church. Through these marks, Christ governs and nourishes his church. We depend on these things as we "look for the resurrection of the dead, and the life of the world to come."

The Nicene Creed closes with those words. The creed sets our eyes on the hope before us, the blessed appearing of our Lord Jesus Christ and the resurrection of the dead. As we trust in Christ, we trust in his promise of new, glorified bodies—and a new creation.

The Nicene Creed, then, is practical. It teaches us the heartbeat of the Christian faith. It teaches us who our God is, what he has done to save us, and how he now works through his church as we wait for the world to come.

The baton has been handed to us. It began with the apostles and comes into our hands 2,000 years later. I hope that you have it in your hand and in your heart. By the grace of God, may you share it with others. May the Lord bless you as you seek to glorify Jesus and hold fast to the rule of faith, the faith once for all delivered to the saints.

Questions for Reflection

1. What are the three marks of the church?

2. What is church discipline? How do you feel about the idea of church discipline?

Notes

Notes

More Church Resources *Available*

LEAD A GROUP WITH
SOLA BIBLE STUDIES

Our growing library of Bible studies will take you deep into God's word in ten lessons. They're perfect for individual use, small groups, Sunday school, and community outreach. Leader's editions are available for all our studies, making it easier for you to lead a group.

New Testament	Old Testament	Topical Studies
Galatians	Daniel	Core Christianity 101
Hebrews	Jonah	How to Read the Bible
John	Ruth	The Nicene Creed
Luke		Parables
Philippians		
Romans		
Revelation		

Written by authors such as Adriel Sanchez, Dennis Johnson, and Andrew Menkis

MORE RESOURCES TO
AID DISCIPLESHIP

Designed to help people find answers to common questions and dig deeper into foundational truths, our booklets are ideal tools for discipleship. Typically less than 100 pages and always written by trusted authors, these booklets provide rich, accessible content for personal reflection.

All Bible Studies and resources are available at store.solamedia.org or by scanning the QR Code.

Booklets

What Is God's Will for Me?

What is Secularization?

Can the Devil Read My Mind?

Law & Gospel

How to Keep Your Faith After High School

Why Would Anyone Get Married?

Seeing Jesus

Made in the USA
Columbia, SC
13 May 2024

35532444R00072